Wild
ALASKAN SEAFOOD

Wild ALASKAN SEAFOOD

Celebrated Recipes from America's Top Chefs

JAMES O. FRAIOLI

FOOD PHOTOGRAPHY BY
JESSICA NICOSIA-NADLER

FOREWORD BY CHEF JOHN ASH

LYONS PRESS
Guilford, Connecticut
An imprint of Globe Pequot Press

To buy books in quantity for corporate use
or incentives, call **(800) 962-0973**
or e-mail **premiums@GlobePequot.com.**

Lyons Press is an imprint of Globe Pequot Press.

Photos by Jessica Nicosia-Nadler unless otherwise credited on p. 263.

Text design: Sheryl P. Kober

Layout: Melissa Evarts

Project editor: John Burbidge

Library of Congress Cataloging-in-Publication Data is available on file.

ISBN 978-0-7627-6047-3

Printed in China

10 9 8 7 6 5 4 3 2 1

To the state of Alaska; to the Alaska Seafood Marketing Institute—an integral part in helping to promote sustainable seafood; to Ed's Kasilof Seafoods—encouraging consumers to purchase sustainable seafood from Alaska; and to all the contributing chefs in this book, whose appreciation for Alaska shines through every dish they prepare.

Contents

Part Three: SHELLFISH, MOLLUSKS, AND OTHERS

Foreword

BY JOHN ASH
James Beard Award–Winning Author and Chef

*M*uch of what is reported in the media is a little depressing when it comes to our oceans. Overfishing, habitat destruction, and pollution seem to dominate the headlines for most articles or reports. Unfortunately much of this is often true, and we can't deny the world's oceans are in crisis in many places around the world.

Along comes Alaska to give us hope. It is the poster child for healthy and sustainable practices in the wild. "Sustainable" in Alaska means the fisheries are actively managed and fished using practices that ensure its seafoods will always be there in the future. It

is, in fact, mandated by law. When Alaska became a state in 1959, its citizens wrote sustainability into their constitution. Enforcement procedures, which include time and area closures, restrictions on size of boats and the fishing gear that they use, along with strict monitoring of catch size and the ability to trace the catch as it is shipped to market, all help to ensure against overfishing. Constant monitoring of ocean and shore habitat also ensures a healthy environment for its seafood.

There are more than forty Marine Protected Areas (MPAs) covering hundreds of thousands of square miles of Alaska's oceans that have been established to safeguard their pristine water habitat from human intervention and pollution. These MPAs not only protect the seafood we enjoy from there but also the whales, sea lions, otters, bird life, and other creatures that coexist there. Proof of the pudding is that no Alaska seafood has ever been listed as endangered under the Endangered Species Act. Quite a testament to the State's commitment.

One reason for the growing popularity of fish and shellfish during the last decade has been the strong evidence from groups such as the National Academy of Sciences and the Harvard School of Public Health that seafood is among the most beneficial foods we can eat. All kinds of reasons are suggested, but among the most important of them are the abundant supplies of omega-3 fatty acids in seafood. These have been shown to be essential for childhood development, help reduce the risk of heart disease, strengthen the immune system, and even possibly help prevent such tragic ailments as Alzheimer's disease.

These are all certainly reasons to eat as much seafood as we can, but my interest has always been to eat them because they are the most delicious foods I can think of. Many home cooks are a little intimidated by cooking seafood, but once you start, you'll find they are generally quick and easy to do. With Alaska as a resource, this then is the reason for this beautiful book of amazingly creative recipes that James O. Fraioli has assembled for all of us to enjoy!

Introduction

*I*f you're a seafood lover, especially one who enjoys pure, natural seafood from sustainable, clean, and healthy fisheries, this book is for you.

Wild Alaskan Seafood is about the very best when it comes to the bounty of the sea. That's because every delicious fish and shellfish featured in this book comes from the icy waters of Alaska—home to the most abundant and well-managed fish stocks in the world. That means you won't find farm-raised, chemically injected salmon or king crab from overfished foreign waters in this book. With the cleanest and most natural marine environments of its size on earth, Alaska stands alone as a model of fisheries management around the globe.

In the beautiful pages ahead, you'll discover more than one hundred signature recipes—all featuring fresh Alaskan seafood—from some of the best chefs in America. There are quick and easy recipes for cooks looking for fast, simple dishes. There are appetizers, soups, and salads for those seeking an interesting side dish to accompany a meal. And there are elaborate recipes for those wanting to prepare something to celebrate a special occasion. There are also dozens of culinary tips and seafood secrets inserted throughout to help take the stress out of fish preparation and storage. After all, cooking seafood should be rewarding and fun.

Depending on where you live, there's a good chance you won't be able to find every fish and shellfish in this book at your local market, and that's okay. Many of the seafood items are interchangeable. If you can't find flounder, use sole. Can't find clams, use mussels. Can't find wild coho salmon, use wild sockeye . . . Keep in mind, however, that with the Internet and airfreight shrinking the globe, you're now able to order fresh Alaskan seafood direct from Alaskan suppliers today, and have a box of deliciousness delivered to your front doorstep tomorrow. It's that easy.

> ## *Did You Know?*
>
> Alaska supplies more than half of all the wild-caught seafood in the United States.
>
> Alaska is home to the greatest wild salmon runs in the world and provides as much as 95 percent of North America's wild salmon.

This book is designed to serve as an inspiration for the modern seafood cook. It's also much more than just a collection of delicious recipes. It is an exciting journey into the undersea world of Alaska. Whether you're a weekend barbecuer or a professional chef, this book is all about learning, selecting, and preparing the best seafood on the market while entertaining your family and friends.

Wild Alaskan Seafood is organized into three parts: Salmon; Deepwater Fish; and Shellfish, Mollusks, and Others. Combined, twenty-three of the most prized fish and shellfish in Alaska are discussed and prepared by twenty-five of America's most decorated chefs, allowing creative and culinary artistry to shine through on every page.

While thumbing through this savory book, take advantage of the opportunity to learn about the best seafood in the world while having fun—just like our featured chefs did while assembling the recipes. Feel free to adjust a seasoning to suit your individual taste, or replace an ingredient with one you find more appealing. There are no steadfast rules, so experimentation and customization are encouraged. And if you get hung up on an unfamiliar ingredient, cooking utensil, or preparation method, there's no need to panic. Today, the Internet is only a click away and available on most cellular phones. That means you're only seconds away from finding the answer to something you did not previously know.

So what are you waiting for? Dive beneath the cold, crisp waters of Alaska and enjoy the exciting culinary experience that awaits!

Part One
SALMON
———

"Michael and Kurt Bohlsen and I are on the same page when it comes to ocean conservation. It is our duty as chefs and restaurateurs to do our part in making sure the ocean continues to feed us for years to come. In our restaurants, we always strive to serve sustainable seafood."

—Chef Cornelius Gallagher

Chapter 1

CHINOOK "KING" SALMON

CHEF CORNELIUS GALLAGHER—THE BOHLSEN RESTAURANT GROUP

The chinook salmon is Alaska's state fish and one of the most important sport and commercial fish species in North America. Also known as king salmon, they are the largest of all Pacific salmon, commonly exceeding 30 pounds.

Chinook are anadromous: hatching in freshwater, spending part of their life in the ocean, and returning to freshwater to spawn. Because chinook mature in inshore marine waters, they are readily available to commercial and sportfishing all year. Catches of chinook in Southeast Alaska are regulated by quotas set under the Pacific Salmon Treaty. In other regions of Alaska, chinook fisheries are closely managed to ensure stocks are not over-harvested.

When purchasing chinook, always select fresh whenever possible, and look for "wild troll-caught king"—the most sustainable choice—as opposed to gill-net or farm-raised salmon.

Chef Cornelius Gallagher, corporate chef for the Bohlsen Restaurant Group, is considered one of the "Best Chefs in America" by *Food and Wine Magazine* and one of "New York's Most Influential Chefs" by *New York Magazine.* As executive chef, he turned Manhattan's Oceana into New York's best seafood restaurant and a top dining destination.

After graduating from the Culinary Institute of America, Chef Gallagher worked in restaurants around the world, including the original Restaurant Bouley, Lespinasse, the three-star Michelin L'Esperance, Peacock Alley, and Daniel. During Chef Gallagher's tenure at Daniel, the restaurant received four stars from the *New York Times,* and Chef Gallagher traveled to "stage" at three-star Michelin El Bulli in Roses, Spain. In his new role as corporate chef, his primary responsibility is enhancing the high-quality customer experience that has become a Bohlsen family signature.

"As an executive chef who is always on the lookout for top-quality ingredients, I find wild king salmon from Alaska to be superior. For years, I have used wild king salmon on my menus, and I find the fish well worth the price. The color of the firm flesh is a natural ruby red, and the flavor profile lends itself well to an assortment of preparations. For me, there is no comparison. With wild Alaskan king salmon, you get what you pay for—quality."

Slow-Cooked King Salmon
with Pickled Chanterelles and Sweet Pea Juices

HOW TO MAKE THE SALMON: Using a very sharp knife, cut the salmon into 4 perfectly even-size pieces and set aside.

In a medium-size saucepot over low heat, simmer the rice vinegar with the sugar, bay leaf, and coriander until sugar is completely dissolved. Place the chanterelles in a bowl and pour the vinegar liquid over them. Let stand at room temperature for at least 1 hour. Drain the chanterelles and discard all the garnish.

Next, bring some salted water to a boil in a large pot. Add the peas and cook until tender. Remove the peas and transfer to a bowl of ice water. When cold, drain the peas and place them in a blender. Add some of the cooking water, melted butter, tarragon, and lime zest. Puree until fine, season to taste, and strain though a fine sieve. Set aside.

In a small bowl, mix the sherry vinegar and the 2 teaspoons olive oil. Toss the pea tendrils lightly in the liquid and set aside.

In a high-sided pot, add the two cups olive oil and heat over low temperature. Season the salmon and add to the oil. Poach the salmon slowly until very small beads of white albumen appear on the surface. Using a slotted spatula, remove the salmon and drain on a paper towel. To test for doneness, insert a cake tester through the center of the fish. If you feel no resistance in the center, it is ready.

HOW TO PLATE: Heat some of the pea sauce and place some in the center of each plate. Add the salmon and chanterelles, and top with the pea tendrils. Serve immediately.

MAKES 4 SERVINGS

2 pounds fresh Alaskan king salmon fillets, skin and blood removed
1/4 cup rice vinegar
3 tablespoons sugar
1 bay leaf
2 teaspoons coriander seeds
1/2 cup chanterelles, cleaned
1 cup English peas, shucked
2 teaspoons whole butter, melted
1 tablespoon sliced tarragon leaves
1 teaspoon grated lime zest
1 teaspoon sherry vinegar
2 teaspoons olive oil
2 cups olive oil
1/4 ounce pea tendrils

Salad of Marinated King Salmon with Heirloom Tomato, Crushed Avocado, Arugula, and Chilled Basil Dressing

For the Tomatoes
1 large heirloom tomato, peeled, cut into 8 wedges, and seeded
1/4 cup peeled and thinly sliced red onion
Olive oil, as needed
3 tablespoons red wine vinegar
2 tablespoons chopped fresh parsley
Pinch salt and pepper

For the Salmon
4 pieces fresh Alaskan king salmon fillets, 6 ounces each

For the Pesto
1/3 cup basil leaves
1/4 cup vegetable oil
2 tablespoons toasted pine nuts
1 clove garlic, peeled
1 tablespoon grated Parmesan cheese

For the Avocado
1 avocado, peeled and seeded
1 teaspoon fresh lemon juice
1 teaspoon cumin powder

1 cup arugula leaves

Note: Begin preparing this recipe 1 day ahead of serving.

How to make the tomatoes: Combine the tomato wedges, red onion, 3 tablespoons olive oil, red wine vinegar, and parsley in a large wooden bowl, toss well, and season with salt and pepper. Cover the bowl tightly with plastic wrap and refrigerate overnight, gently stirring the tomatoes frequently. The following day, drain the tomatoes, reserving the juices and tomatoes separately. Set aside.

How to make the salmon: Fill a medium saucepan halfway with olive oil and heat over a medium flame. When the oil is hot, add the salmon and cook the fillets until the flesh begins to turn color and the salmon begins to form very small white beads of albumen at the base. When you can run a cake tester through with little resistance, it's done. Immediately, remove the salmon from the heat and place the fillets on a large dinner plate. Splash them with the reserved tomato marinade juices and cover with plastic wrap. Leave at room temperature.

How to make the pesto: In a blender, combine the basil, vegetable oil, pine nuts, garlic, and Parmesan cheese; cover and puree until smooth. Add some of the reserved tomato marinade juice to the pesto. The resulting pesto should be a sauce consistency. Chill until ready to serve.

How to make the avocado: In a medium-size mixing bowl, combine the avocado with the lemon juice and cumin, and season to taste with salt and pepper. Crush the avocado lightly with the back of a fork, mixing until just combined.

HOW TO PLATE: Spoon the avocado into the center of four chilled dinner plates. Arrange the salmon on top of the avocado, and spoon the reserved tomato pieces atop each piece of salmon. Drizzle the chilled basil-tomato marinade puree around the plate, and garnish with some arugula leaves.

MAKES 4 SERVINGS

"When cooking fresh king salmon, lower temperature and slower cooking are always better. If you cook salmon too fast, an unappealing white matter [known as albumen] will form on the edges of the fish. To know when salmon is properly cooked, simply run a cake tester or toothpick through the center. When there is almost no resistance, the fish is ready to come off the heat and rest for a few minutes before serving."

Smoke-Poached King Salmon with Marinated Cucumbers and Melted Yogurt Dressing

HOW TO MAKE THE SALMON: In a medium saucepot, heat the butter until melted. Add the onions and caramelize them slowly until a deep brown color is obtained, approximately 30 minutes. Add the chicken stock and simmer 10 minutes longer. Strain and finish with salt, pepper, and Liquid Smoke. Add this liquid to a shallow pot, and set aside.

In a medium bowl, whisk together the vinegar and oil. Add the cucumber, piquillo peppers, and dill. Allow to marinate at room temperature for at least 2 hours. Chill.

In a separate saucepan, over low heat, melt the yogurt and add the cardamom and pepper. Season to taste with salt and pepper.

Heat the smoke-onion bouillon in the shallow pot you had set aside to about 135°F (use a candy thermometer to measure temperature, or heat the broth until you can only hold your finger in for 3 seconds). Add the fish and poach until small beads of albumen begin to form on the surface of the fish. Check the doneness of the fish with a cake tester. Keep warm.

HOW TO PLATE: Lay out four small plates. Dress each plate with some of the yogurt dressing. In the center of each, lay some of the cucumbers. Top with the hot fish, and serve immediately.

MAKES 4 SERVINGS

4 tablespoons butter
2 white onions, peeled and sliced
3 cups chicken stock
2 teaspoons Liquid Smoke hickory seasoning
2 tablespoons red wine vinegar
2 tablespoons olive oil
1 European cucumber, peeled and cut in thin julienne
2 piquillo peppers, roasted, peeled, seeded, and julienned
1 tablespoon fresh dill, washed and sliced
½ cup organic yogurt
¼ teaspoon ground green cardamom
1 teaspoon black pepper, freshly ground
Pinch sea salt and white pepper, to taste
4 3-ounce fillets fresh Alaskan king salmon

> "Chinook salmon have the highest oil content of all five species of wild salmon."

King Salmon Roasted in Phyllo with Pea Shoots, Bean Sprouts, Cactus Pear Juice, and Spicy Mustard Oil

For the Salmon
2 3-ounce king salmon fillets, skinless, bloodline removed
Pinch salt and white pepper
$1/3$ cup phyllo dough, shredded
4 tablespoons whole butter

For the Vegetables
1 tablespoon vegetable oil
$1/2$ cup fresh bean sprouts, cut in 2-inch segments
$1/2$ cup fresh pea shoots, cut in 2-inch segments
2 teaspoons sesame oil
2 teaspoons white soy sauce

For the Sauce
$1/3$ cup cactus pear juice (also known as prickly pear)
2 tablespoons passion fruit juice
1 tablespoon chopped cilantro (coriander) leaves
3 tablespoons spicy mustard oil (available at Asian markets)

HOW TO MAKE THE SALMON: Season the fish with salt and white pepper and press one side gently into the phyllo. Heat the butter and sauté the salmon, phyllo side down, until crispy and golden. Remove from heat, and transfer to a baking sheet, phyllo side up. Reserve in a 200°F oven until ready to serve.

HOW TO MAKE THE VEGETABLES: Heat the vegetable oil and lightly sauté the bean sprouts and pea shoots until tender. Season to taste and finish with the sesame oil and soy.

HOW TO MAKE THE SAUCE: In a small pot, heat the pear and passion fruit juices, cilantro, and mustard oil until simmering.

HOW TO PLATE: Spoon sauce onto two serving plates. Divide and lay the vegetables in the center and top with the salmon.

MAKES 2 APPETIZER SERVINGS

"When buying king salmon, always look for resilient flesh, clear eyes, and bright red gills. These are indicators the fish is fresh. Touch the salmon's outer skin. The fish should feel slimy (this slime helps the fish propel itself through the water, and is another indicator of freshness)."

Herb-Roasted King Salmon with Parmesan Egg, Country Bacon, and Farmer's Vegetable Broth

For the Potage
¼ pound unsalted butter
2 leeks, sliced finely crosswise
2 carrots, peeled and cut into small chunks
1 rib celery, peeled and cut into small chunks
2 turnips, peeled and diced small
3 ounces smoked bacon, diced large
1 bay leaf
1 head green cabbage, chiffonade then finely chopped
1 cup green beans, cut in ³/₄-inch segments cooked until soft
5 fingerling potatoes, peeled and cut into small chunks

For the Roasted Salmon
¼ cup olive oil
4 6-ounce fillets fresh Alaskan king salmon
1 tablespoon chopped shallots
2 tablespoons chopped thyme leaves

For the Parmesan Cream
1 tablespoon grated Parmesan
¼ cup crème fraiche
2 tablespoons mascarpone cheese
Juice 1 lemon
Salt and pepper to taste
4 eggs, poached

HOW TO MAKE THE VEGETABLES: In a medium pot, melt the ¼ pound butter. Add the leeks, carrots, celery, and turnips. Season with some salt and sweat slowly for 5 minutes. Add 1 quart of water and bring to a boil. Add the bacon, bay leaf, and cabbage; cover and simmer slowly for approximately 40 minutes. Remove the bacon, small dice it, and return it to the soup with the cooked green beans. Add the potatoes and simmer until just cooked, about 15 minutes. Keep the broth warm while you prepare the salmon.

HOW TO MAKE THE SALMON: In a medium pan, heat the olive oil and pan-roast the fish until golden on both sides. Add the shallots and thyme to the pan. Tilt the pan and baste it with the herb oil. Keep the fish warm while you prepare the cream.

HOW TO MAKE THE CREAM: In a small pot, heat the Parmesan, crème fraiche, and mascarpone. Boil and strain the melted cheese through a fine sieve. Season to taste with the lemon, salt, and pepper.

HOW TO PLATE: In the center of four large dinner bowls, ladle 4 ounces of the farmer's broth (with the vegetables). Place the fish in the center. Top the fish with a poached warm egg and spoon the cream over the top. Serve immediately.

MAKES 4 SERVINGS

"My first job after culinary school was at a seafood restaurant in Port Jefferson, Long Island. We [the cooks] used to hold a competition to see who could break down a salmon the fastest, from whole to portioned. I did it in ninety seconds. As I got older and wiser, I realized speed has nothing to do with good cooking, so my advice to home cooks is never rush. Take your time and enjoy the process. In addition to the competition, one of the reasons I was able to fillet salmon so quickly was because the pin bones were easy to remove. That's not a good thing. Easy-to-remove pin bones is an indicator of a less-than-fresh fish. Something I learned later in life."

David Anderson
Executive Chef

"There are many reasons to use sustainably sourced seafood. First, we need to immediately take the pressure off those wild species that are in serious decline due to overfishing. As a business that sells seafood, we need to rethink what we sell, and consumers need to rethink what they purchase. In addition, many of the farmed species of both fish and shellfish are not sustainably farmed, making the problems worse. We do use certain farm-raised fish but strictly limit these to the approved 'Green-listed' Monterey Bay Aquarium Seafood Watch species. When consumers stop buying products that are not sustainable, the pressure ultimately changes the entire industry."

—Executive Chef David Anderson

Chapter 2

CHUM "KETA" SALMON

EXECUTIVE CHEF DAVID ANDERSON—THE PORTOLA CAFE

Chum salmon, also known as Keta salmon, are the most abundant commercially harvested salmon species in Alaska and have the widest distribution of Pacific salmon. Unfortunately, they rarely share the stage with the more desirable salmon such as chinook and sockeye.

Because of their low market value compared to other salmon, chum are considered the least commercially viable species. But don't let that fool you. An ocean-going chum salmon is excellent table fare and a great value for the money. The meat is firm with a tempting light orange-pink color and delicate flavor. As with all salmon, chum are an excellent source of protein and extremely low in saturated fats. If you like a more mild-flavored wild salmon, try chum salmon from Alaska waters.

> "Keta salmon, or chum salmon, as it's commonly called, is a mild yet flavorful salmon. Alaskan Keta is a readily available product with a great price point, making it an attractive product for our restaurant."

As the executive chef of Portola Cafe at the Monterey Bay Aquarium, Chef David Anderson lets the seasons and the Seafood Watch Program dictate the menus with fresh, local ingredients taking center stage. Prior to joining the aquarium as executive chef, Chef Anderson studied at the Culinary Institute of America in Hyde Park, New York, and went on to work at two of the top ten restaurants in Philadelphia. One of these restaurants was voted by *Bon Appetit* magazine as one of the top new restaurants in the United States.

While working as executive sous chef of Bittersweet Bistro in Aptos, California, Chef Anderson became conscious that menus can be based on local, sustainable ingredients. He took this lesson to heart, and since then, his commitment to local and sustainable ingredients has shaped his many successful cooking ventures.

Grilled Keta Salmon with Zinfandel Jelly, Parsnip-Fennel Puree, Tuscano Kale, and Applewood-Smoked Bacon

For the Zinfandel Jelly
1 750-milliliter bottle Zinfandel
1½ cups water
7 cups sugar
1 pouch liquid pectin

For the Parsnip-Fennel Puree
1 medium onion, medium dice
1 large bulb fennel, green top removed and medium dice
3 pounds parsnips, peeled and medium dice
3 tablespoons butter
Chicken stock, as needed
2 cups milk
Kosher salt and white pepper, as needed

For the Braised Tuscano Kale
¼ pound applewood-smoked bacon, short julienne
3 bunches fresh Tuscano kale, cleaned, stems removed, and chiffonade
Kosher salt and white pepper, as needed

For the Salmon
6 fillets fresh Alaskan chum salmon
Olive oil, as needed
Kosher salt and pepper, as needed

HOW TO MAKE THE ZINFANDEL JELLY: Combine the wine, water, and sugar in a large stockpot. Bring to a boil. Add the pectin and return to a rolling boil for 1 minute. Jelly can be canned at this point and stored for up to 1 year or cooled and reserved.

HOW TO MAKE THE PARSNIP-FENNEL PUREE: Sauté the onions, fennel, and parsnips in butter until light brown. Add the chicken stock, milk, kosher salt, and pepper. Simmer until tender. In a blender puree the solids, adding only enough liquid to form a smooth puree.

HOW TO MAKE THE TUSCANO KALE: Starting in a cold sauté pan, slowly cook the bacon until the fat has rendered out and is crisp. Add the kale and cook until wilted. Season with kosher salt and pepper.

HOW TO MAKE THE SALMON: Lightly coat the salmon with olive oil and season with the salt and pepper. Grill the salmon on a hot, clean grill for 4 minutes on each side, turning 90 degrees at the 2-minute mark on each side. Remove from heat.

HOW TO PLATE: Brush the salmon with the Zinfandel jelly while still hot and divide among serving plates alongside the kale and parsnip-fennel puree.

MAKES 6 SERVINGS

"I was not always a fan of eating seafood. When I was younger, I was exposed mainly to frozen fish, and this turned me off to seafood. As I started my working life, I was waiting tables in an oceanside restaurant that billed itself as having the freshest seafood in the area. As a representative of the restaurant, I felt it was my duty to know what I was selling to the guests and begrudgingly set out to eat my way through the entire menu. From the beginning, I realized there was a big difference between the fish of my youth and what they were serving. From that point forward I fell in love with seafood, its variety of tastes and textures and versatility in preparation. Today, in addition to fresh sustainably farmed species, I have suppliers that offer frozen-at-sea fish that is far superior to what was available in the past, so I can serve high-quality wild Alaskan salmon even out of season."

Keta Salmon on Brioche with Caramelized Onion Marmalade, Meyer Lemon Aioli, Arugula, and Pickled Vegetable Slaw

For the Pickled Vegetables

1 quart unseasoned rice wine
  vinegar
1/2 cup sugar
3 tablespoons crushed chili
  flakes
1/4 cup kosher salt
3 cups julienned carrots
1 1/2 cups julienned red bell
  pepper
1 1/2 cups julienned kohlrabi

For the Meyer Lemon Aioli

1 cup canola oil
2 whole garlic cloves, peeled
1 slice brioche, crust removed
2 tablespoons dijon mustard
Zest 1 Meyer lemon
Juice 1 Meyer lemon
2 egg yolks
1/4 cup white wine

For the Caramelized Onion Marmalade

3 tablespoons canola oil
2 large yellow onions,
  julienned
1/4 cup white balsamic
  vinegar
1/4 cup white port wine

For the Salmon

6 4-ounce fillets fresh
  Alaskan keta salmon
12 slices brioche, lightly
  toasted
6 ounces arugula
Pinch kosher salt and white
  pepper, to taste

How to make the pickled vegetables: Combine the vinegar, sugar, chili flakes, and salt. Bring to a boil. Allow to cool slightly then pour over the carrots, peppers, and kohlrabi and allow to cool. Serve chilled.

How to make the Meyer lemon aioli: In a small saucepot, combine the oil and garlic and simmer over medium-low heat until the garlic is light brown and soft; cool and reserve. In a food processor or blender, process the bread into crumbs; add the mustard, zest, juice, egg yolks, and wine. With the machine running, slowly add the oil and garlic to form a mayonnaise.

How to make the caramelized onion marmalade: Starting in a cold sauté pan, combine the oil and onions and cook over medium-low heat, stirring occasionally, until the onions are very soft without adding color. Add the vinegar and wine and reduce to a syrup. Cool and reserve.

How to make the salmon: Sear the salmon on both sides, cooking to medium.

How to plate: Spread the aioli on one side of each of the slices of brioche. Lay out 6 brioche slices, top each with a salmon fillet, then top with the marmalade and arugula. Top with the remaining 6 brioche slices. Serve with the pickled vegetables. (Note: The sandwich can also be assembled without toasting the brioche and grilled using a panini press.)

MAKES 6 SERVINGS

Keta Salmon Blanquette Crepes with Pinot Noir Gastrique

For the Pinot Noir Gastrique
¼ cup water
1 cup sugar
½ cup red wine vinegar
½ cup Pinot Noir

For the Crepe Batter
2 large eggs
1 cup milk
1 cup flour
4 tablespoons cornstarch
1 teaspoon powdered ginger
1 teaspoon kosher salt
¼ pound butter, melted

For the Salmon Blanquette
4 ounces butter
2 ounces oyster mushrooms, torn into small pieces
1 small yellow onion, diced small
1 small celery root, peeled and diced small
1 parsnip, peeled and diced small
¾ cup flour
2 cups chicken stock
2 tablespoons minced fresh thyme
¼ cup minced flat-leaf parsley
Zest 2 lemons
⅔ cup cream
Pinch kosher salt and pepper, to taste
1½ pounds fresh Keta salmon, skin removed and diced to ¼ inch

HOW TO MAKE THE PINOT NOIR GASTRIQUE: In a very clean medium-size saucepan, add the water. Add the sugar to the middle of the pan without letting it get onto the sides. Bring the sugar mixture to a boil over high heat; do not stir. If sugar crystals form on the sides of the pot, brush them down with the water. Cook the sugar until it turns light brown; at this point you can gently swirl to evenly cook the sugar. Add the vinegar and Pinot Noir using caution: The sugar is very hot and may splatter. Dissolve the sugar and reduce the mixture by half. Cool to room temperature and reserve.

HOW TO MAKE THE CREPE BATTER: In a blender add the eggs and milk. In a separate bowl sift together the flour, cornstarch, ginger, and salt. Combine the flour mixture and the egg mixture in the blender and blend while slowly adding the melted butter. Blend only long enough to incorporate the butter. Allow to rest for 1 hour. Next, heat a 10-inch nonstick pan over a medium flame. Lightly coat with nonstick spray and add 2 ounces of batter. Swirl slowly to coat the entire bottom of the pan. Cook for 2 minutes or until the crepe releases easily from the pan, then flip and continue cooking 1 more minute. Continue with the remaining batter. Note: This recipe should produce more than the 6 crepes required. Keep crepes warm until ready to serve.

How to make the salmon blanquette: Melt the butter (note: this will seem like a lot of butter, but it is a part of the roux that will be made later in the same pan). Add the mushrooms and onions. Cook slowly until the onions are translucent. Add the celery root and parsnips and sauté for 3 minutes. Add the flour, stirring well to incorporate it into the butter, and continue cooking for 5 minutes, stirring constantly. Whisk in the chicken stock and bring to a simmer; cook for 10 minutes to remove the flavor of raw flour. Add the herbs, lemon zest, and cream, return to a simmer, and season with kosher salt and pepper. Add the salmon and simmer for 3 minutes or until the salmon is ¾ cooked through.

How to plate: Fill each warm crepe with ½ cup of the salmon filling. Fold up the sides, overlapping to form a square pouch. Turn over on a plate with the seams on the bottom. Drizzle with Pinot Noir sauce and serve immediately.

MAKES 6 SERVINGS

"When preparing Keta salmon at home, be careful not to overcook it. Keta salmon does not have the same fat content as, say, king salmon, so Keta tends to dry out. Also, try to pair Keta salmon with items that will add moisture to the dish, such as fresh vegetable purees or glazes."

Keta Salmon En Papillote with Baby Spinach, Roasted New Skin Potatoes, Root Vegetables, and Fresh Herbs

For the Roasted New Skin Potatoes
1½ pounds Yukon gold or red skin potatoes, quartered lengthwise
3 tablespoons canola oil
3 shallots, peeled and quartered
Pinch kosher salt and pepper, to taste

For the Root Vegetables
3 tablespoons canola oil
2 cups peeled and medium-diced candy stripe beets
2 cups peeled and medium-diced carrots
2 cups peeled and medium-diced rutabaga
Pinch kosher salt and pepper, to taste

For the Salmon En Papillote
6 15 x 36-inch sheets parchment paper
½ cup olive oil
1 pound baby spinach, washed
6 5-ounce fillets Keta salmon
¼ cup minced garlic
½ cup minced shallots
1 cup white wine
¼ cup minced fresh dill
¼ cup minced fresh parsley
Pinch kosher salt and pepper, to taste

HOW TO MAKE THE POTATOES: Preheat the oven to 450°F. In a large sauté pan over medium-high heat, sauté the potatoes in oil until they are golden brown. Add the shallots, and season with kosher salt and pepper. Roast in the oven for 15 minutes or until the potatoes are fork tender. Allow to cool. (Leave the oven at 450°F for the next step.)

HOW TO MAKE THE ROOT VEGETABLES: In a large sauté pan, heat the oil and sauté the beets, carrots, and rutabaga until they start to brown. Season with kosher salt and pepper. Finish in the oven (450°F) until the vegetables are fork tender, about 15 to 20 minutes. Allow to cool and reserve.

HOW TO MAKE THE SALMON EN PAPILLOTE: Preheat the oven to 500°F. Fold each piece of parchment paper in half and cut it into the shape of a half heart with the seam at the center. Drizzle 2 tablespoons of olive oil on the inside of each of the sheets of parchment paper and close to spread evenly. Open the parchment and layer the spinach, potatoes, vegetables, salmon, garlic, shallots, white wine, and herbs, and then season with salt and pepper. Starting opposite of the point of the heart, start to fold the parchment to form a balloon. Overlap each fold until you have completely sealed the package. Repeat with the remaining papillotes. Brush the top of each papillote with a little oil to protect from scorching and bake for 10 minutes.

HOW TO PLATE: Remove from oven and divide among serving plates. Open carefully with a sharp knife or scissors, protecting yourself from escaping steam.

MAKES 6 SERVINGS

Sweet Potato–Crusted Keta Salmon with Sprouted Broccoli, Roasted Fingerling Potatoes, and Citrus Sabayon

For the Sweet Potato Crust
3 orange sweet potatoes, peeled and shredded on cheese grater
2 quarts canola oil

For the Roasted Fingerling Potatoes
1¹/₂ pounds French fingerling potatoes, halved lengthwise
3 tablespoons canola oil
3 shallots, peeled and quartered
Pinch kosher salt and pepper, to taste

For the Citrus Sabayon
3 egg yolks
¹/₄ cup white wine
Zest and juice 1 lime
Zest and juice 1 lemon
3 tablespoons honey
1 bunch fresh chives, minced

For the Salmon
3 large eggs
2 tablespoons dijon mustard
6 5-ounce fillets fresh Keta salmon
Pinch kosher salt and pepper, to taste
3 bunches fresh broccolini

HOW TO MAKE THE SWEET POTATO CRUST: Squeeze the excess liquid from the sweet potatoes. Heat the oil in a 4-quart stockpot to 300°F. Fry the potatoes until they just change to light brown.

Remove from the oil and drain on an absorbent cloth until cool. The potatoes should be crisp at this point.

HOW TO MAKE THE ROASTED FINGERLING POTATOES: Preheat the oven to 450°F. In a large sauté pan over medium-high heat, sauté the potatoes in oil until they are golden brown. Add the shallots and season with kosher salt and pepper. Roast in the oven for 15 minutes, or until the potatoes are fork tender. (Leave the oven heated at 450°F for the salmon.)

HOW TO MAKE THE CITRUS SABAYON: Add 3 inches of water to a medium saucepan and bring to a simmer over medium heat. Combine the eggs, wine, lime zest and juice, lemon zest and juice, and honey in a stainless steel bowl that fits on the top of the saucepan. Cook the mixture over the simmering water until it thickens, stirring constantly with a whisk. Finish with the minced chives and hold in a warm spot.

> "I would always recommend that you purchase your salmon from a shop that does not smell like fish and has brisk sales. This will help ensure that your fish is fresh. . . .
>
> Always keep your purchase as cold as possible. If you are more than 10 minutes from the market, have your salmon packed in a plastic bag with ice."

HOW TO MAKE THE SALMON: Combine the eggs and mustard. Season the salmon fillets with kosher salt and pepper and brush the tops with the egg mixture. Gently press the fillets into the sweet potato crust and arrange on a lightly greased baking sheet. Bake the salmon for 5 to 7 minutes (450°F) or until medium. Steam the broccolini for 3 minutes in boiling salted water.

HOW TO PLATE: Arrange the potatoes on the plate with the broccolini on top followed by the salmon and sabayon.

MAKES 6 SERVINGS

"I had the opportunity to see one of the management tools for the salmon fishery in action just outside of Juneau. It was a fish wheel located on the Taku River about a mile from the Canadian border. Operating from a small shoreline camp, officials were using a device that had been used by native fishermen to capture and tag salmon as they swam upstream to spawn. It was a netted wheel that spun with the current, trapping the fish from behind as they made their way through the eddies. As they were caught, the salmon were funneled into a well from which they were gently removed, measured, tagged, and recorded. The fish were released back into the water to continue their journey. It was an exciting experience to help with this process as you could feel the strength and power of these fish as I held them to measure them. It is very rare that we have the opportunity to engage with a fish while it is still a fish, meaning not being turned into seafood. As a seafood chef, I have had more than my fair share of experiences with fillets, but a living fish in its own river, that was pretty cool."

—Executive Chef Barton Seaver

Chapter 3

Coho Salmon

Executive Chef Barton Seaver—National Geographic Ocean Fellow

*C*oho salmon, also called silver salmon, are found off the Pacific, particularly in Washington, Canada, and Alaska.

In North America, salmon fishermen catch about 25,000 tons of wild coho each year. The majority of this harvest comes from Alaska, where coho are fished from July to September. About 40 percent of the North American coho harvest is caught by trollers, the preferred method of fishing compared to nets. Troll-caught, frozen-at-sea (FAS) coho are considered the highest quality coho you can buy. Although not as highly regarded as king or sockeye, coho can be a great salmon for the money.

Some wild coho runs have a reputation for producing softer-fleshed fish than other runs. However, the softness is a function of how well the fish was handled, not the waters from which it came.

As a graduate of the prestigious Culinary Institute of America, Chef Barton Seaver has been at the helm of some of Washington, D.C.'s most acclaimed restaurants. After bringing the idea of sustainable seafood to D.C. in an award-winning setting at Hook restaurant in Georgetown, he later opened Blue Ridge restaurant, where Chef Seaver continued garnering recognition, including *Esquire* magazine's 2009 Chef of the Year.

Chef Seaver has been lauded as a leader in sustainability by Seafood Choices Alliance. He was recently named a Fellow with the Blue Ocean Institute, and he also works with the National Geographic Society. Locally, Chef Seaver is an appointed member of the Mayor's Council on Nutrition in Washington, D.C., where he is helping to craft a wellness policy for District residents.

Coho Salmon with Quinoa Pilaf
and Toasted Almond Herb Butter

For the Salmon Brine
2 cups cold water
1½ tablespoons kosher salt
1 tablespoon sugar
4 5-ounce fillets fresh coho
   "silver" salmon

For the Quinoa Pilaf
2 tablespoons extra-virgin
   olive oil
1 small onion, diced
3 tablespoons raisins
2 cups quinoa
4 cups water
Pinch salt, to taste

For the Herb Butter
2 tablespoons unsalted
   butter (room temperature)
2 tablespoons chopped fresh
   parsley
1 tablespoon chopped
   almond slivers, toasted in a
   350°F oven for 5 minutes
1 fresh lemon, juiced
Pinch salt, to taste

HOW TO MAKE THE SALMON: Prepare the brine by combining the cold water, salt, and sugar, stirring to dissolve. Next, add the fish to the liquid, making sure that it is covered. Allow to sit in the refrigerator for 15 to 20 minutes. Remove the fish from the brine and pat dry with paper towels. Brush with olive oil and place in an oven-proof dish. Place the fish in a 275°F oven and bake for 20 to 25 minutes. Be careful not to overcook.

HOW TO MAKE THE QUINOA PILAF: In a large saucepan, heat the olive oil and add the diced onion. Sauté on medium heat until the onion begins to soften. Add the raisins and sauté for another 2 minutes. The raisins should lightly caramelize with the onions. Add in the quinoa and turn to high heat. Continue to cook until the quinoa begins to turn an amber-brown color and develops a nutty aroma. Add the water, bring to a boil, and then reduce heat to low. Season with salt and stir. Cover and simmer for 20 minutes or until all of the water is absorbed.

HOW TO MAKE THE HERB BUTTER: Combine the butter with the chopped parsley, almond slivers, and lemon juice. Season with salt and mix well with a fork. Keep at room temperature until ready to serve.

HOW TO PLATE: For each plate, evenly divide the quinoa pilaf and place a salmon fillet directly on top. Spoon a small amount of the butter over the top of the fish and serve immediately.

MAKES 4 SERVINGS

"Because coho has a delicate flavor and a moderate fat content, I find the best way to prepare coho is cook it slowly. You will notice when I roast fish it is done in a low-temp oven. When I sauté, I go for moderate heat that ensures the fish will stay moist and flavorful. I also brine nearly every piece of seafood I serve. The simple and quick task adds so much flavor and richness to the final dish that it is very worth the time."

Coho Salmon with Sweet Potato Salad with Cinnamon Vinaigrette

For the Salmon Brine
2 cups cold water
1½ tablespoons kosher salt
1 tablespoon sugar
4 5-ounce fillets fresh coho "silver" salmon

For the Sweet Potato Salad
2 large sweet potatoes
Cold water, as needed
1 small onion, diced
Pinch salt, to taste
Zest 1 orange
2 tablespoons mayonnaise

For the Cinnamon Vinaigrette
1 shallot, diced
3 tablespoons olive oil
1 teaspoon cinnamon powder
2 teaspoons chopped fresh oregano
Juice 1 orange
2 tablespoons red wine
Pinch salt and fresh cracked pepper, to taste
Fresh watercress or arugula leaves, for garnish

HOW TO MAKE THE SALMON: Prepare the brine by combining the cold water, salt, and sugar, stirring to dissolve. Next, add the fish to the liquid, making sure that it is covered. Allow to sit in the refrigerator for 15 to 20 minutes. Remove the fish from the brine and pat dry with paper towels. Brush with olive oil and place in an ovenproof dish. Place the fish in a 275°F oven and cook for 20 to 25 minutes. Be careful not to overcook.

HOW TO MAKE THE SWEET POTATO SALAD: Leave the skin on the potato and cut it into bite-size pieces. Place in a pan and cover with cold water. Add the diced onion and season with salt. Place on the burner and bring to a boil. Potatoes should be done just as it boils so check a couple pieces with a knife. If the tip pierces easily, strain the potatoes and allow to cool slightly. Next, place the potatoes and onions in a bowl and toss with the orange zest and mayonnaise. Try not to break the potatoes too much. You don't want to end up with a puree, but rather a nice chunky salad lightly dressed with the mayonnaise.

HOW TO MAKE THE CINNAMON VINAIGRETTE: Sauté the shallot in the olive oil over medium heat. Cook until the shallot is just soft, about 2 minutes or so. Add in the cinnamon and oregano and stir to incorporate. Cook for 1 minute to develop its flavor. Add in the orange juice and red wine. Cook until the smell of alcohol is removed and the sauce has been reduced by about half. Season with salt and a few turns of fresh cracked pepper.

HOW TO PLATE: Place a fillet of salmon over a mound of the warm potato salad. Garnish with a few sprigs of watercress or arugula. Spoon the vinaigrette over the top of the salmon and serve immediately.

MAKES 4 SERVINGS

"When we talk about seafood we talk about many hardworking families who rely on the oceans for their livelihood. We, in turn, rely on these communities to help protect and manage our coasts and some of the most important cultural heritage that we have in this country. I like to know when I buy seafood from a sustainably managed fishery, I am helping to support a relationship with our oceans that spans centuries and many generations. In Alaska, it is very common to see multiple generations of a family all working together, and I like to sell their story to my guests. It creates the same connection we often find with local farmers that is so often missing when it comes to seafood."

Sautéed Coho Salmon
with Caraway-Scented Beans and Herb Salad

HOW TO MAKE THE SALMON: Prepare the brine by combining the cold water, salt, and sugar, stirring to dissolve. Next, add the fish to the liquid, making sure that it is covered. Allow to sit in the refrigerator for 15 to 20 minutes. Remove the fish from the brine and pat dry with paper towels. Next, in a large pan on medium heat, add 1 tablespoon butter and melt until the butter begins to foam. Add the salmon fillets and reduce the heat to low. Allow to cook for 8 minutes and then gently turn. Turn off the heat on the pan and allow the salmon to finish cooking from the residual heat. Just before serving, re-warm the salmon on medium heat for 1 minute.

HOW TO MAKE THE BEANS: In a small saucepot, melt the ½ tablespoon butter and add the ground caraway seeds. Toast the spice for 30 seconds then add the drained beans and chicken stock. Bring to a simmer and gently crush a few of the beans using the back of a spoon. This will slightly thicken the stock. When the stock has been reduced by half, add in the cream cheese and stir to melt and incorporate. Season with salt and reserve.

HOW TO MAKE THE HERB SALAD: Mix the mint and parsley with the sliced onion, dress with the lemon juice, and season with salt. Toss to combine.

HOW TO PLATE: Ladle the beans into large bowls and place a salmon fillet on top. Garnish each dish with a generous portion of the herb salad and serve immediately.

MAKES 4 SERVINGS

For the Salmon Brine
2 cups cold water
1½ tablespoons kosher salt
1 tablespoon sugar
2 5-ounce fillets fresh coho "silver" salmon
1 tablespoon butter

For the Caraway-Scented Beans
½ tablespoon butter
2 teaspoons ground caraway seeds
2 10-ounce cans navy beans, drained
2 cups chicken stock
3 ounces cream cheese
Pinch salt, to taste

For the Herb Salad
1 bunch fresh mint, leaves picked
1 bunch fresh flat-leaf parsley, leaves picked
1 small onion, sliced extremely thin
Juice ½ lemon
Pinch salt, to taste

Smoked Coho Salmon Chowder

8 ounces hot-smoked coho salmon (purchase prepackaged)
3 cups cold water
2 tablespoons butter, divided
1 medium onion, diced
1 teaspoon ground coriander
3 medium russet potatoes, diced into 1/2-inch cubes
1 cup cream
1 tablespoon chopped fresh dill
2 tablespoons chopped fresh parsley
Pinch salt, to taste

HOW TO MAKE THE SALMON CHOWDER: Start by making a very simple salmon broth. Place the smoked salmon in a saucepan with the cold water. Place over medium heat and barely bring to a simmer. Allow to cook on low heat for about 10 minutes, until the salmon is softened and the water has taken on the flavor of the fish. Strain and reserve both the broth and the fish.

Place 1 tablespoon butter in a large pot and place over medium heat. When the butter is melted, add the diced onion and cook until the onion is soft, about 2 minutes. Add in the coriander and stir to incorporate. Add the reserved salmon broth and potatoes to the pan and bring to a simmer. Once the potatoes are cooked, about 4 minutes, add in the cream and lightly mash some of the potatoes using the back of a spoon. This will slightly thicken the soup as the cream reduces. Continue to cook over medium heat for 5 minutes, making sure not to boil it or the cream will curdle. Gently flake the smoked salmon into the soup and stir to incorporate. Allow to sit for 10 minutes before serving for the flavors to meld together.

While the soup is resting, combine the chopped dill with the parsley and the remaining tablespoon of butter. Season with salt and mix well with a fork.

HOW TO PLATE: Serve the soup in bowls and place a dollop of herb butter into the center of each bowl.

MAKES 2 TO 4 SERVINGS

"I believe coho is the most balanced in flavor of all of the salmon species. The fish has a bright clean flavor with a hint of the wild as found in sockeye salmon. Coho is full-flavored but matches well with nearly any preparation. I tend to cook vegetable-heavy dishes where there is a small amount of protein, and coho works well for this, as its flavor carries through the entire dish while not being an oversize portion. Coho also tends to be very reasonably priced, so coho makes for a great weeknight meal."

Coho Salmon Sautéed with Zucchini and Squash

HOW TO MAKE THE SALMON: Prepare the brine by combining the cold water, salt, and sugar, stirring to dissolve the salt and sugar. Next, add the fish to the liquid, making sure that it is covered. Allow to sit in the refrigerator for 15 to 20 minutes. Remove the fish from the brine and pat dry with paper towels. Next, in a large pan on medium heat, add 1 tablespoon butter and melt until it begins to foam. Add the salmon fillets and reduce the heat to low. Allow to cook for 8 minutes and then gently turn. Turn off the heat on the pan and allow the salmon to finish cooking from the residual heat. Just before serving, re-warm the salmon on medium heat for 1 minute.

HOW TO MAKE THE VEGETABLES: Slice the roasted garlic head in half along its equator, gently squeeze out the cloves and reserve. Place a large sauté pan over high heat. Melt 1 tablespoon of butter until it foams, and add the squash and zucchini. Cook on high heat until the vegetables begin to color. Add in the roasted garlic and stir to combine. Continue to cook for another minute and then add the pecan pieces and the water. Stir to combine and add the remaining ½ tablespoon butter. As the butter melts and the water reduces, the vegetables will develop a thin glaze as the butter incorporates; this will take about 2 minutes. Remove from heat and add the chopped mint and onion slices. Toss to combine and serve immediately.

HOW TO PLATE: Evenly divide the vegetables between the plates. Scrape any remaining pan juices from the vegetables over the salmon and serve immediately.

MAKES 4 SERVINGS

For the Salmon Brine
2 cups cold water
1½ tablespoons kosher salt
1 tablespoon sugar
4 5-ounce fillets fresh coho "silver" salmon
1 tablespoon butter

For the Vegetables
1½ tablespoons butter, divided
2 small yellow squash, sliced into half moons
2 small zucchini, sliced into half moons
1 head garlic, wrapped in foil and baked at 325°F for 45 minutes
4 tablespoons chopped pecans
2 tablespoons water
4 sprigs fresh mint leaves, chopped
1 small onion, sliced very thin

"Our Border Grill and Ciudad customers look forward to the middle of May every year when the popular Copper River salmon is available fresh for 3 to 4 weeks. This salmon has a rich flavor that can stand up to strong heat and bold, assertive flavors, and it's loaded with omega-3 fatty acids, which are essential for a healthy diet."

—Chef/Owners Mary Sue Milliken and Susan Feniger

Chapter 4

COPPER RIVER SALMON

CHEF/OWNERS MARY SUE MILLIKEN AND SUSAN FENIGER —BORDER GRILL AND CIUDAD

*I*n Alaska, there is a 300-mile stretch of river considered to be the longest and most rugged of all rivers—the Copper River. The salmon that enter this relentless river to spawn are some of the strongest and most robust fish on the planet. To prepare for their arduous journey, the salmon must store extra oils and body fat, and it's these extra supplements that make Copper River salmon some of the richest and tastiest fish in the world. For the health conscious, this is one time where the fattier the meat, the better it is for you, as Copper River salmon are loaded with omega-3 oils.

Copper River king and Copper River sockeye are the two species that commonly make the journey up the heralded river in a short three- to four-week span each May. Because the commercial harvest season is so short, the price for Copper River salmon is the highest among the species. If you're lucky enough to try fresh Copper River salmon, you are in for a real treat.

Chefs Mary Sue Milliken and Susan Feniger, two of America's most beloved chefs, are hands-on owner-operators of the popular and critically acclaimed Border Grill (both the restaurant and their new venture, the Border Grill Truck) as well as Ciudad restaurant.

Business partners for over twenty-five years, Mary Sue and Susan are prolific in many media outlets. They are authors of five cookbooks, including *Cooking with Too Hot Tamales*, *Mesa Mexicana*, and *City Cuisine*. They are television veterans, starring in almost 400 episodes of Food Network's popular *Too Hot Tamales* and *Tamales World Tour* series, along with Bravo's *Top Chef Masters*. Since 1996, they have had several homes on the radio dial in Los Angeles, including KCRW, KFWB, and KFI. In addition, Border Grill and Ciudad dishes starred in the 2001 Samuel Goldwyn feature film *Tortilla Soup.*

"When cooking fish, you always want to err on the side of undercooking. Fish will continue to cook for 3 to 4 minutes after it leaves the grill or pan. You can always cook underdone fish a little more, but once it is overcooked you cannot get that silky texture back. When cooking a fillet, we start skin-side up on the heat source and then flip it and cook it the rest of the way. That way, you can simply place the fish on the plate so the skin is on the bottom."

Home-Smoked Copper River Salmon
with Fennel, Olive, and Orange Salsa

HOW TO MAKE THE BRINE: Combine the salt, onion, brown sugar, bay leaves, mustard seeds, ginger, peppercorns, allspice, cloves, and water in a medium saucepan (do not add the ice cubes and cold water). Bring to a boil and strain into a ceramic or glass roasting pan. Now add the ice water, and chill. When cool, marinate the Copper River salmon in the brine for 15 minutes at room temperature.

HOW TO MAKE THE HOME-SMOKED SALMON: Make a stovetop smoker with that big old pot you've been meaning to throw away. (Or line a good pot with aluminum foil to keep it from aging quickly.) Place the hickory chips in the bottom of the pot and place a rack above them. Place the pot on a burner over high heat. When chips start smoking, place the salmon on the rack, cover, and cook over moderate heat for 10 minutes. Transfer the salmon to a platter, cover with plastic wrap, and chill.

HOW TO MAKE THE FENNEL, OLIVE, AND ORANGE SALSA: Peel the oranges and cut the segments, trimming between the membranes to remove the sections. Work over a small bowl to catch the juice. Dice the orange segments and add to the bowl. Add the fennel, red onion, jalapeños, black olives, olive oil, lemon juice, and parsley, and mix well. Add the salt and pepper, and adjust the seasoning as necessary.

HOW TO PLATE: Line six serving plates with lettuce leaves, placing a chilled salmon fillet in the center of each plate. Top with the fennel, olive, and orange salsa and serve.

MAKES 6 SERVINGS

For the Brine
1/3 cup coarse salt
1/2 onion, sliced
3 tablespoons brown sugar
3 bay leaves
1 tablespoon mustard seeds
1 1-inch piece fresh ginger, sliced thinly
1 teaspoon black peppercorns
1/4 teaspoon whole allspice
1/4 teaspoon whole cloves
1 cup water
1 cup packed with ice cubes and cold water

For the Salmon
6 6-ounce fillets fresh Copper River salmon
1 cup hickory chips, soaked in water for 1 hour
Lettuce leaves, for garnish

For the Fennel, Olive, and Orange Salsa
2 medium navel oranges
1–2 fennel bulbs, trimmed, halved, and thinly sliced (about 2 cups)
1/2 small red onion, quartered and thinly sliced
2 jalapeños, stemmed, seeded, and minced
1/2 cup kalamata or good-quality black olives, pitted and roughly chopped
1/4 cup extra-virgin olive oil
2 tablespoons freshly squeezed lemon juice
1/2 bunch parsley, chopped
Salt and freshly ground black pepper, to taste

Copper River Salmon Skewers
with Avocado-Tomatillo Dipping Sauce

For the Salmon Skewers
3 tablespoons cumin seeds
3 jalapeños, stemmed, cut in half, and seeded if desired
2 cloves garlic
2 teaspoons freshly ground black pepper
1 teaspoon salt
3 tablespoons freshly squeezed lime juice
1 bunch cilantro
3/4 cup extra-virgin olive oil
6 pickling or Kirby cucumbers, ends trimmed and peeled
2 pounds fresh skinless Copper River salmon fillets

For the Avocado-Tomatillo Dipping Sauce
1 pound tomatillos, husked, washed, and cut into quarters (about 8 to 10 tomatillos)
2-4 large jalapeños, stemmed, seeded if desired, and roughly chopped
1/2 cup freshly squeezed orange juice
3-4 scallions, white and light green parts only, chopped
1 large bunch cilantro, chopped
2 teaspoons salt
2 medium avocados, halved, seeded, and peeled

HOW TO MAKE THE SALMON SKEWERS: Lightly toast the cumin seeds in a dry skillet over low heat just until their aroma is released, about 4 to 5 minutes. Transfer the seeds to a blender. Add the jalapeños, garlic, black pepper, salt, and lime juice, and puree until the cumin seeds are finely ground. Then add the cilantro and olive oil and puree until smooth.

Next, cut the cucumbers in half lengthwise and then slice across the width into 1/2-inch half moons (note: pickling or Kirby cucumbers are small, pale green cucumbers with fewer seeds and a milder flavor than larger cucumbers). Sprinkle lightly with salt, gently toss, and let sit in a colander for 20 to 30 minutes, allowing excess water to drain.

Meanwhile, cut the salmon into 1½-inch chunks and place in a bowl. Pour the jalapeño cilantro marinade over the salmon, toss, and let sit 20 to 30 minutes.

Preheat the grill or broiler. Thread alternating salmon and cucumber chunks on wood or metal skewers. Grill or broil about 1½ minutes per side.

HOW TO MAKE THE AVOCADO-TOMATILLO DIPPING SAUCE: Place the tomatillos, jalapeños, and orange juice in a blender. Puree just until chunky. Add the scallions, cilantro, salt, and avocados and puree about 2 minutes more, or until smooth.

HOW TO PLATE: Place the salmon skewers on a large plate and serve immediately accompanied by the avocado tomatillo dipping sauce.

MAKES 6 SERVINGS

"Ever since chef's school, where commonly there was only one salmon for forty students to practice filleting, we have been fascinated with using the whole fish. We were taught to use the bones to make stock, the fillets for main courses, and the scraps from scraping the bones for mousse or pate. We used to entertain guests at our first CITY restaurant by waltzing through the dining room with a whole fish on our arms and a squirt-gun through its mouth. We were mesmerized by the beauty of the creature and wanted to show it off before filleting."

Cold Poached Copper River Salmon with Tomato and Herbs

HOW TO MAKE THE SALMON: Preheat the oven to 350°F. Season the salmon with salt and pepper. In a large ovenproof skillet, bring the stock or clam juice to a boil. Add the salmon fillets, so they are barely touching, and bring the liquid back to a boil. Turn the fillets over, and cover with a piece of parchment paper coated with olive oil. Transfer the skillet to the oven and bake for 5 minutes. Turn the fillets over, cover again, and bake an additional 2 minutes. (Drain and reserve the liquid in the pan for use as stock.) Transfer to a platter, cover with plastic wrap, and chill until serving time.

HOW TO MAKE THE TOMATO AND HERBS: Remove stems from the mint, basil, and parsley, then finely chop the remaining leaves, along with the chives. (Note: Other herbs that work well include chervil, fennel fronds, cilantro, oregano, dill, watercress, and celery leaves.) Combine the herbs with the tomatoes, olive oil, sherry, salt, and pepper in a small bowl and reserve in refrigerator.

HOW TO PLATE: Arrange each fillet on a lettuce-lined serving plate. Spoon the tomato and herbs over the fish. Garnish with sliced avocado, radishes, pickles, or olives around the salmon.

MAKES 6 SERVINGS

For the Salmon
6 6-ounce fillets fresh skinless Copper River salmon
Salt and freshly ground black pepper, to taste
3 cups fish stock or clam juice

For the Tomato and Herbs
1 bunch mint
1 bunch basil
1 bunch parsley
1 bunch chives
6 tomatoes, cored, seeded, and diced
$\frac{1}{2}$ cup extra-virgin olive oil
2 tablespoons Spanish sherry wine vinegar
$1\frac{1}{2}$ teaspoons salt, to taste
$\frac{1}{4}$ teaspoon freshly ground black pepper
Lettuce leaves, for serving
Sliced avocado, radishes, pickles, and/or olives, for serving

Grilled Copper River Salmon Tacos with Cucumber Citrus Salsa

For the Salmon
1½ pounds fresh Copper River salmon fillets
Extra-virgin olive oil, for drizzling
Salt and freshly ground black pepper, to taste
12 6-inch corn tortillas

For the Cucumber Citrus Salsa (makes 3 cups)
1 orange
1 grapefruit
1 lime
4 pickling cucumbers, diced
½ small red onion, diced
½ bunch cilantro, chopped (about ⅓ cup)
1 teaspoon salt
½ teaspoon freshly ground black pepper
2 serrano chilis, stemmed and sliced in thin rounds
6 lettuce leaves
2 avocados, halved, seeded, peeled, and diced, for serving
Radish slices, for serving
Lime wedges, for serving

How to make the salmon: On the stovetop, heat a grill pan over medium-high heat, or prepare a medium-hot fire in a charcoal or gas grill. Drizzle the salmon with olive oil, season with salt and pepper, and grill until barely done, 2 to 5 minutes per side, depending on the thickness. Remove the salmon from the grill, let cool slightly, and pull apart into large flakes. Meanwhile, dip corn tortillas in water, shaking off excess. Toast, in batches, in a nonstick pan over moderate heat, about 1 minute per side. Wrap in a towel to keep warm.

How to make the cucumber citrus salsa: Slice ends off the orange, grapefruit, and lime and stand upright on a counter. Cut away the peel and membrane, exposing the fruit. Working over a bowl to catch the juices, separate the citrus sections by slicing with a knife between the membranes. Remove and discard the seeds. Cut the citrus segments into small dice and add to the bowl with all the juices. Add the cucumbers, red onion, cilantro, salt, pepper, and serrano chilis. Toss well and let sit, covered, at least 30 minutes. (Note: You can store this salsa in the refrigerator up to 48 hours.)

How to plate: Place the tortillas on a work surface. Line each tortilla with a piece of lettuce and top with chunks of fish. Top each with a generous spoonful of cucumber citrus salsa and a drizzle of olive oil. Serve with avocado, radish, and lime wedges.

MAKES 4 SERVINGS

Copper River Salmon Chowder with Cilantro Pesto

For the Chowder

2 tablespoons unsalted
  butter
1 medium onion, diced
1 large carrot, peeled and cut
  into 1/4- to 1/2-inch dice
1 stalk celery, cut into 1/4- to
  1/2-inch dice
1 large potato, peeled and
  cut into 1/4- to 1/2-inch dice
1/2 teaspoon salt
1/4 teaspoon freshly ground
  black pepper
2/3 cup dry white wine
4 cups clam juice
1 cup heavy cream
1 cup milk
1/2 tablespoon softened,
  unsalted butter
1 tablespoon all-purpose
  flour
1 1/2 pounds fresh Copper
  River salmon, cut into
  1-inch pieces
2 dashes Tabasco
Juice 1/2 lemon

For the Cilantro Pesto

2 bunches cilantro, roughly
  chopped
Juice 2 limes
2 tablespoons extra-virgin
  olive oil
2 tablespoons water
1/2 teaspoon salt

HOW TO MAKE THE SALMON CHOWDER: Melt the 2 tablespoons of unsalted butter in a large stockpot over medium heat. Add the onion and cook until soft, about 5 minutes. Add the carrot, celery, potato, salt, and pepper and cook an additional 3 minutes, stirring occasionally to avoid browning. Add the wine and clam juice and bring to a boil, cooking 5 minutes or until reduced by half. Add the cream and milk, return to a boil, and then reduce to a simmer. Cook over medium-low heat, uncovered, until the vegetables are tender, about 10 minutes.

Combine the 1/2 tablespoon of soft unsalted butter with the flour, using your fingers to form a smooth paste. Press the paste on the ends of a whisk and stir into the soup until completely and evenly dispersed. Add the salmon pieces and continue to simmer, about 10 to 15 minutes, or until fish is just cooked through. Stir in the Tabasco and lemon juice. Taste and adjust seasonings as necessary.

HOW TO MAKE THE CILANTRO PESTO: Place the cilantro, lime juice, olive oil, water, and salt in a food processor or blender, and mix until a paste is formed.

HOW TO PLATE: Divide the chowder among serving bowls and top with a spoonful of cilantro pesto.

MAKES 6 SERVINGS

"We fell in love with seafood when we were young, and we want our children and grandchildren to have the same opportunity including plenty of choices. Seventy percent of seafood eaten in the United States is served in restaurants, and as chefs, we feel it is our responsibility to provide our guests with fish that are not threatened by extinction or raised in ways that damage the ocean's ecosystems. By partnering with Monterey Bay Aquarium and Alaska Seafood Marketing Institute, we have learned so much about the oceans and sustainable seafood and we are grateful they keep us informed about which fisheries and species we can proudly say are sustainable."

"As a long-standing member of SSI [Sustainable Sea-food Initiative], we at Hank's feel it is important to take measures to ensure the continued sustainability of immediate ecosystems and oceans as a whole. It's amazing how much fish we process each day, and we're just one restaurant. The demand being placed on the species is making it impossible to reproduce at a sustainable rate. It requires vigilance on our part. I feel it is important to implement a well-balanced management system that can work for everyone."

—Chef Frank McMahon

Chapter 5

SOCKEYE SALMON

CHEF FRANK MCMAHON—HANK'S SEAFOOD

*I*n the wild salmon business, this is the money fish. More than three-quarters of the world sockeye harvest comes from Alaska, and in a good year, almost 80 percent of the value of the state's total salmon harvest is of sockeye. Although most of the North American sockeye harvest is exported, there's a growing appetite for this great-tasting salmon in the Lower 48.

The quality of sockeye (and other wild salmon) will vary within the same run; early in the run, fish will generally be brighter and have more oil as they have to migrate farther upriver. The price of sockeye can vary for a number of reasons, including the method of capture. The most expensive sockeye are landed in a small troll fishery while seine-caught fish are also of premium quality and command a premium price. The least expensive sockeye are caught in Bristol Bay, where only gillnets can be fished.

After his studies at the Culinary Institute of America and an externship in Germany, Chef Frank McMahon returned to the United States to work at New York's famed Le Bernardin. Having begun to refine a signature less-is-more style that focused on the subtleties of flavors, Chef McMahon was recruited to open Opus Restaurant in Santa Monica as sous chef, and in 1992 it was named one of America's "Best New Restaurants" by *Esquire*.

After moving to Charleston, South Carolina, Chef McMahon worked as executive chef at Restaurant Million and McCrady's and later at Elliott's on the Square. In 1998 he, along with several colleagues, opened Hank's, a modern interpretation of a Charleston fish house. The successful juxtaposition of seafood platters and traditional low-country dishes and more creative culinary influences is the result of Chef McMahon's dedication to a simplicity that affects an evolution of flavors on the palate.

"What I like best about fresh sockeye salmon from Alaska is its versatility in the kitchen, its distinct flavor profile, its delicious and healthy fat content, and its radiant color."

Grilled Sockeye Salmon with Roasted Garlic–Lemon–Smoked Olive Oil Emulsion

HOW TO MAKE THE EMULSION: Combine the sliced onions, the roasted garlic puree, and chicken stock in a small stockpot and simmer until onions are tender. Add the lemon juice. Pour the mixture into a blender and puree at high speed. During the blending, slowly add the olive oil and champagne vinegar. Season with salt and pepper and strain the emulsion through a fine sieve.

HOW TO MAKE THE SALMON: Simply grill the salmon on high heat until medium rare.

HOW TO PLATE: Finish with frisée, apple-smoked bacon bits, and roasted fingerling potatoes.

MAKES 4 SERVINGS

½ large white onion, thinly sliced
2 tablespoons roasted garlic puree (found in specialty stores or at www.igf-inc .com)
2 cups chicken stock
4 ounces lemon juice
3–4 ounces smoked extra-virgin olive oil (found in specialty stores or at www .igf-inc.com)
1 ounce champagne vinegar
Pinch salt and pepper
4 6- or 7-ounce fresh sockeye salmon fillets
Frisée
Apple-smoked bacon bits
Roasted fingerling potatoes

"When serving fresh salmon, try not to complicate the dish. Less is more. Keep it simple."

Salmon Rillettes

1 pound fresh sockeye
   salmon fillet
2 ounces white vermouth
Pinch salt and pepper
2 tablespoons mayonnaise
2 tablespoons finely diced
   shallots
2 tablespoons sour cream
½ lemon, juiced
1 teaspoon fresh chopped
   chervil
1 teaspoon fresh chopped
   chives
1 teaspoon fresh chopped
   tarragon
Crostini
Cucumber twists, for garnish

How to make the salmon: Cut the salmon into 2-inch squares, and lay on a half sheet pan. Sprinkle the vermouth, salt, and pepper over the fish. Place into a 400°F oven for 5 minutes. Salmon should be medium rare. Drain any liquid from sheet pan and reserve.

Place salmon in a bowl. Break the salmon pieces with a fork. Let rest until cool.

In a pan over medium-high heat, add the reserved liquid from the sheet pan, reduce the liquid by half, and cool. When cool, add the liquid to the salmon, along with the mayonnaise, shallots, sour cream, lemon juice, chervil, chives, and tarragon. Toss well.

How to plate: Serve the salmon in a shallow dish along with crostini. Garnish with thinly sliced cucumber twists.

MAKES 8 SERVINGS

> "Open your mind to cooking salmon medium or medium rare, with an opaque center."

"There's an old Irish fable I recall from my childhood days, which I often think about when preparing sockeye salmon. I'm Irish by birth, so the tale is a part of our heritage. The story is about a poet who sits by the river waiting to catch the salmon of knowledge. The first person to taste the fish would become the wisest in Ireland, but many could not catch the fish. Eventually after many attempts, the poet caught the fish but had a friend cook the fish. After a drop of salmon oil landed on the friend's hand, it was not the poet but his friend who would become the wisest in the land."

Oven-Roasted Sockeye Salmon
with Horseradish–Grain Mustard Vinaigrette

How to make the horseradish–grain mustard vinaigrette: Place both mustards in a bowl. Slowly whisk in a portion of the combined oils to start the emulsion. As the emulsion forms and thickens, dilute with a little of the combined vinegars. Then alternate back and forth until all the oils and vinegars are incorporated to achieve a smooth emulsion. Whisk in the horseradish and season with salt and pepper.

How to make the salmon: Preheat the oven to 500°F. In a large nonstick pan over high heat, add canola oil. Heat until the oil begins to ripple. Season the salmon fillets with salt and pepper. Place the salmon skin-side down in the pan and sear for 2 minutes. Transfer the pan to the oven, and continue to cook skin-side down for approximately 5 minutes. Remove the pan from the oven and flip the salmon skin-side up.

How to plate: Present the salmon skin side up, and spoon the vinaigrette around the fish. Accompany the dish with heirloom potatoes and grilled asparagus.

MAKES 4 SERVINGS

For the Horseradish–Grain Mustard Vinaigrette
2 tablespoons dijon mustard
1 tablespoon whole-grain mustard
7 ounces canola oil
2 ounces extra-virgin olive oil
1 tablespoon hazelnut oil
1 tablespoon walnut oil
1 1/2 ounces sherry vinegar
1 1/2 ounces balsamic vinegar
1 1/2 ounces red wine vinegar
1 tablespoon prepared horseradish
Pinch salt and pepper

For the Oven-Roasted Salmon
1 tablespoon canola oil
4 6- or 7-ounce fillets scaled skin-on fresh sockeye salmon
Pinch salt and pepper

"Take advantage of skin-on fillets by crisping them skin-side down."

Sockeye Salmon Tartare

2 pounds fresh sockeye
    salmon
Pinch salt and pepper
1 tablespoon extra-virgin
    olive oil
1 ounce fish sauce
1 garlic clove, finely chopped
1 lemon, zested
1 tablespoon chopped
    shallots
1 tablespoon fresh chopped
    chives
1 tablespoon fresh chopped
    tarragon
1 tablespoon fresh chopped
    chervil
1 tablespoon fresh chopped
    cilantro
2 tablespoons seeded,
    skinned, and finely diced
    tomato
Micro greens, for garnish
Taro chips

HOW TO MAKE THE SALMON TARTARE: Finely dice the salmon, making sure that it is free of any bloodline or cartilage. Season the salmon in a bowl with salt and pepper. Add the olive oil, fish sauce, garlic, and zest. Toss, and add the shallots, chives, tarragon, chervil, cilantro, and tomato.

HOW TO PLATE: Serving options can be to mold the tartare in a cylinder form-quenelle or spread thinly on a plate. Garnish with micro greens and serve with taro chips.

MAKES 8 SERVINGS

"Fishy flavor can come from overcooking. The best method is preparing and serving your salmon lightly cured or raw. . . .

Always ask to smell the salmon. There should never be an offensive odor, but a pleasant aroma of melon and cucumber."

Home-Cured Sockeye Salmon with
Watermelon-Cucumber-Mint Vinaigrette

For the Salmon

2–3 pounds fresh center-cut
  sockeye salmon fillets
2 cups kosher salt
1/4 cup sugar
1 tablespoon fresh chopped
  mint
1 tablespoon fresh chopped
  chervil
1 tablespoon fresh chopped
  cilantro
1 tablespoon fresh chopped
  arugula
1/4 cup water

For the Watermelon
Vinaigrette

1 small seedless watermelon
Fresh cracked black pepper
  and pinch kosher salt
2 cloves garlic, chopped
1 red onion, diced
1 seedless English cucumber
1 bunch fresh mint, julienned
  or thinly sliced
1 tablespoon black sesame
  seeds
4 ounces champagne
  vinegar

HOW TO MAKE THE SALMON: Ensure that the salmon fillet is free of cartilage, pin bones, and bloodline. In a bowl, combine the kosher salt, sugar, mint, chervil, cilantro, arugula, and water and toss well. Using a kitchen brush, coat the salmon thoroughly with the herb paste. Place the coated salmon in the refrigerator for 2 hours. After marinating in the refrigerator, remove the salmon and thoroughly wash the paste from the fish. Pat the salmon dry with paper towels and place back in the fridge.

HOW TO MAKE THE WATERMELON VINAIGRETTE: Dice 4 cups watermelon and juice the rest of the watermelon. Heat and reduce the watermelon juice by half. Chill the juice and reserve. To the watermelon, add the pepper, salt, garlic, and onion. Thoroughly mix and add the cucumber, mint leaves, sesame seeds, and vinegar, along with the reserved juice.

HOW TO PLATE: Thinly slice the cured salmon and allow 4 to 5 slices per person. Arrange the slices on a plate, carpaccio style. Finish with the watermelon vinaigrette and garnish with mint leaves.

MAKES 6–8 SERVINGS

> "Use a skewer to test internal temperature. Zero resistance means the fish is overcooked. Slight resistance means the salmon is perfect!"

Part Two

DEEPWATER
FISH

"I love fresh Alaskan black cod for a number of reasons. The meat is firm, flakey, moist, and sweet, and just enough good oils to increase the way the flavors remain on the tongue. Black cod is one of those great fish that creates a seafood memory because of its flavor relation to halibut. The deeper white fish of these cold waters have a texture and flavor that accommodates cooking techniques from sauté, steam, grill, and fry. Black cod can also absorb any sauce or vegetable into the wonderfully adaptable meat."

—Chef H. Lamar Thomas

Chapter 6

BLACK COD (SABLEFISH)

CHEF H. LAMAR THOMAS—CHEF LAMAR'S IRON GRILL

One of the market names for sablefish—"butterfish"—says it all. Exceptionally rich and flavorful, sablefish is the most expensive bottomfish landed by U.S. fishermen. Although more than 90 percent of the sablefish catch is exported to Japan, a growing number of chefs in the United States are learning to appreciate the buttery taste and texture of this fish.

Along with Pacific halibut, sablefish are managed in Alaska by an individual fishing quota (IFQ) system, which allows individual longline fishermen to harvest a predetermined amount of fish anytime during the spring to fall season. These sablefish are caught in deeper, colder water and command a higher price as they have a higher oil content, firmer texture, and are much larger than those caught off the West Coast. As a result, Alaska produces about 75 percent of the 30,000 to 40,000 tons of sablefish caught off North America every year.

With Chef Lamar Thomas at the helm, the East West Bistro opened in the spring of 1995 with the idea of blending Pan Asian and Mediterranean cuisines into one great concept that has become a trademark of American cuisine. Recently, Chef Thomas opened Chef Lamar's Iron Grill in Athens, Georgia.

Chef Thomas has lived in, worked in, and visited many places in the United States as well as other parts of the world. Having spent time in the Southeast, Northern California, the Outer Banks, Michigan, and China, he has developed an understanding and appreciation of local foods and cuisines and believes that food is the great communicator between cultures within and from without any geographical region.

Chef Thomas is the author of *A Romance with Food: Ginger, Lily and Sweet Fire*, and has two more cookbooks in production. He is also a regular writer of two food columns for *Southern Distinction* and *Atlanta Cuisine* magazines.

"The first experience I had with black cod was discovering it smoked at the Mendocino coast at the wonderful St. Orres Inn. To this day, black cod is one of the best smoked fish. In the 1980s, black cod was unavailable fresh, so eating smoked cod was how I was introduced to the species."

Fried Black Cod Seasoned with Bacon and Apple Slaw, Sweet Potato Fries, and Sweet Chili Mayonnaise

How to make the bacon and apple slaw: Combine the cabbage, pickles, bacon, apples, red onion, garlic, sesame seeds, parsley, olive oil, and vinegar. Mix well and refrigerate.

How to make the sweet potato fries: Slice the sweet potatoes into steak fries. In a bowl, place the water, and add the salt. Soak the fries in the salted water and refrigerate for 3 to 5 hours, or overnight. Heat the oil in a deep iron skillet or home fryer to 350°F. Drain and pat dry the sweet potato fries. Fry in the oil until crisp. For best results, fry in small batches, not all at once. Also, do not let the oil temperature drop more than 15 degrees when adding the fries. If the oil remains hot, the fries will be crispy. If the temperature drops too low, the fries will be soggy.

How to make the sweet chili mayonnaise: Simply whisk the mayonnaise, sweet pickles, hot sauce, sugar, and curry powder until well combined. Refrigerate.

How to make the black cod: Dust the cod in the flour and tempura batter. Drizzle the tempura with the water and move the fish around so that the coating is sticky. Dust again with tempura batter. Then deep fry (as you did the sweet potato fries but in new oil) after the fry oil has reached 350°F. Add the cod pieces one by one, allowing 15 seconds in between. Fry for 8 minutes. Remove and drain.

How to plate: Arrange the black cod on individual serving plates. Stack the sweet potato fries next to the fish. Top the fish with a tablespoon of sweet chili mayonnaise. The apple-bacon slaw can either go on top of the black cod or on the side.

MAKES 4 SERVINGS

For the Bacon and Apple Slaw
- 1/2 cup shredded green cabbage
- 1/4 cup diced sweet pickles
- 6 ounces (raw weight) apple-smoked bacon, cooked crisp in iron skillet and chopped
- 2 Golden Delicious apples, diced
- 1/3 cup diced red onion
- 1 tablespoon minced garlic
- 1 teaspoon sesame seeds
- 2 tablespoons chopped fresh parsley
- 1/4 cup olive oil
- 1/4 cup white balsamic vinegar (or champagne vinegar)

For the Sweet Potato Fries
- 3 large sweet potatoes
- 1 quart cold water
- 1 tablespoon kosher salt
- 1 quart corn or peanut oil

For the Sweet Chili Mayonnaise
- 1 cup mayonnaise
- 2 tablespoons diced sweet pickles
- 1 teaspoon hot sauce
- 1 teaspoon sugar
- 1 teaspoon curry powder

For the Black Cod
- 4 6-ounce black cod fillets
- 1 cup all-purpose flour
- 1 cup tempura batter
- 5 tablespoons cold water

Grilled Black Cod with Blackberries and
White Wine Butter Sauce

For the White Wine Butter Sauce
½ cup white wine
1 teaspoon cranberry juice
2 tablespoons minced shallots
1 tablespoon apple cider vinegar
1 bay leaf
6 ounces cold butter, cut into small pieces
¼ teaspoon sea salt
¼ teaspoon ground white pepper

For the Black Cod
4 7-ounce black cod fillets, at least 1 inch thick
20 seedless grapes, halved
20 fresh blackberries
¼ cup toasted cashews

HOW TO MAKE THE WINE BUTTER SAUCE: Combine the white wine, cranberry juice, shallots, cider vinegar, and bay leaf, and reduce on medium heat until liquid is merely a shine on the shallots. Truly, this must be reduced to barely a tablespoon of liquid. Next, keep the pan on the warm surface and whisk the cold butter cuts into the pan piece by piece. Only whip in one piece at a time. Do this until all the butter is incorporated into the sauce. Strain through a fine strainer, season with salt and pepper, and keep in a warm, not hot, place. If the sauce gets too hot, it will break; if it gets too cold, it will solidify and then break when it touches the hot fish. If the butter is not melting and combining quickly enough with the shallots, move the pan back and forth over the warm stovetop. From start to finish, this sauce should take about 15 minutes.

HOW TO MAKE THE BLACK COD: On a hot outdoor barbecue or indoors under the broiler, grill the fish until moist and slightly translucent, being careful not to overcook.

HOW TO PLATE: Divide the cod on four serving plates. Pour a few tablespoons of the wine butter sauce over the fish. Top with fresh grapes, blackberries, and the toasted cashews.

MAKES 4 SERVINGS

Oven-Fried Black Cod with Lime–Coconut Milk Sauce

For the Pan Sauce
1 cup thick-sliced mushrooms
1 tablespoon butter
1 lime, zested and juiced
1 cup coconut milk
1 teaspoon soy sauce
1 teaspoon Worcestershire
   sauce
1/3 teaspoon cayenne pepper

For the Shoestring Vegetables and Noodles
1 zucchini
1 carrot
1 yellow squash
10 fresh basil leaves
1 lemon, juiced
1 cup cooked angel hair pasta
1/4 cup water

For the Egg Wash
2 tablespoons dijon mustard
1 teaspoon mayonnaise
6 tablespoons all-purpose
   flour
4 eggs, beaten
1 egg white, beaten with eggs

For the Black Cod
Italian-style bread crumbs, as
   needed
1 cup all-purpose flour
20 1½-ounce cubes black cod,
   4 per plate
Seaweed salad, for garnish
Walnuts, for garnish
Red and orange bell pepper,
   for garnish

How to make the pan sauce: In a pan over medium-high heat, sauté the mushrooms in the butter and set aside. In a separate pan, combine the lime, coconut milk, soy sauce, Worcestershire, and cayenne pepper. Return the pan to the heat and reduce the sauce by half (note: sauce will be thick). Add the mushrooms, stir, and set aside.

How to make the shoestring vegetables and noodles: Cut the vegetables on a microplane cutter or on the zesting side of a box grater. Thinly slice the basil and add to the vegetables. Squeeze lemon juice over the vegetables. Add the cooked pasta, stir, and set aside. Just before serving, steam the vegetables and pasta in a small pan with ¼ cup water for 3 minutes.

How to make the egg wash: Whisk the dijon, mayonnaise, and flour with the eggs and egg white. This wash enables the breading to stick to the fish and make it crispy.

How to make the black cod: Set up three plates, one filled with flour, one with the egg wash, and one with bread crumbs. (Note: Keep your left hand for the wet and your right hand for the dry at all times.) Place the cod into the flour and coat the fish. Transfer to the egg wash. Cover with the mixture. Transfer to the bread crumbs and make sure all the cubes are completely covered.

Place the fish on a baking sheet and cook it for 15 minutes at 450°F. Turn over once while cooking. Remove from oven.

How to plate: Divide the cold pasta and vegetables between four plates, in the center of each plate. Divide the mushroom sauce onto the same plates, with four dots of the sauce on each plate. Put the oven-fried black cod on each dot of sauce. Place seaweed salad into the center of the oven-fried-fish circle. Sprinkle with walnuts. Garnish with sliced rings of sweet red and orange peppers.

MAKES 4 SERVINGS

Sautéed Black Cod and Virginia Ham with Steamed Spinach and Sweet Onion Relish

For the Corn Bread

This is up to you and your favorite buttermilk corn bread recipe—the corn bread enhances a dish that crosses the continent from old South Georgia to modern-day Alaska. You will need four 2-ounce squares for this dish.

For the Onion Relish

2 sweet yellow onions, sliced
2 tablespoons diced Poblano peppers
¼ cup light brown sugar
¼ cup light soy sauce
1 tablespoon grated fresh ginger

For the Spinach

8 ounces fresh spinach
1 ounce rice vinegar

For the Black Cod

4 5-ounce black cod steaks, thick cut
1 tablespoon corn oil
1 tablespoon extra-virgin olive oil
¼ cup all-purpose flour
4 pieces precooked ham (each approximately 3 inches by 3 inches)

HOW TO MAKE THE ONION RELISH: Combine the onions, peppers, brown sugar, soy sauce, and ginger. Place in roasting pan, cover, and bake at 375°F for 20 minutes. Uncover and let cool.

HOW TO MAKE THE SPINACH: Simply steam the spinach with rice vinegar until wilted.

HOW TO MAKE THE BLACK COD: In a sauté pan over medium heat, add corn and olive oils. Dust the cod with flour and add to the pan when the oil is hot. Sear the fish and belly. Transfer the sauté pan to a preheated 400°F oven and finish uncovered for 10 minutes.

HOW TO MAKE THE HAM: Heat four ham squares in a pan on high heat, browning each side.

HOW TO PLATE: On each of four plates, place a piece of corn bread on the bottom, then the black cod, then the ham, and then top with the relish. Lay the steamed spinach next to the corn bread. Squeeze fresh lime over each plate, and serve immediately.

MAKES 4 SERVINGS

> "Today, black cod is available fresh and fresh frozen at sea. If you can only find frozen cod, simply cook it while frozen. If you thaw the fish, you will lose all the juices, and it's the oil and juices that contain the flavor."

"We are the top predator species; it is our job to promote the continued work toward well-managed fisheries and agriculture. Most importantly, good fisheries guarantee great food, which in turn guarantees great restaurants and chefs."

Steamed Black Cod, Artichoke Hearts, Black Olives, and Roasted Red Bell Pepper

How to make the potatoes: Combine the potatoes, garlic, onions, sea salt, pepper, and melted butter, and toss well. Transfer the potatoes to a baking sheet and roast in a 400°F oven for 30 minutes. Keep the potatoes in a warm oven until ready to serve; this should be no more than 15 minutes.

How to make the black cod: Combine the black cod, artichoke hearts, bell peppers, black olives, white wine, Worcestershire sauce, salt, and olive oil, and toss well. Transfer to a deep pan and cover. Steam over high heat for 10 minutes. Do not move the top. The pan must be completely contained. If you do lose some of the steam, cook for a couple additional minutes.

How to plate: After the cod is cooked, divide the pieces among four serving dishes, and top with the pan ingredients. Garnish with orange and grapefruit sections, and serve with a side of the potatoes.

MAKES 4 SERVINGS

For the Potatoes
- 2 pounds Yukon gold potatoes, washed and roughly chopped
- 4 cloves garlic, peeled and mashed
- 2 onions, thick diced
- 1 tablespoon coarse sea salt
- 1 tablespoon coarse black pepper
- ½ cup melted butter

For the Black Cod
- 4 6-ounce fillets black cod
- 16 artichoke hearts
- 4 red bell peppers, quartered
- 16 black olives, no pits
- ½ cup white wine
- 2 tablespoons Worcestershire sauce
- 1 teaspoon salt
- 1 ounce extra-virgin olive oil
- 1 orange, peeled and segmented, for garnish
- 1 grapefruit, peeled and segmented, for garnish

"I love the clean taste and large flakes of lingcod. Its mild flavor makes it a versatile background for flavors both subtle and vibrant."

—Chef Christine Keff

Chapter 7

LINGCOD

CHEF CHRISTINE KEFF—FLYING FISH

Lingcod is a commercially and recreationally important groundfish inhabiting the west coast of North America, with a strong abundance in Alaska. Because lingcod are fast-growing and mature early, they are moderately resilient to fishing pressure. Alaska commercially targets lingcod using hook and line gear, making the Alaskan lingcod a sustainable fishery, further proven by stable lingcod stocks.

Lingcod is available year-round, but the greatest appearance is in spring and summer. Lingcod is marketed as fresh or frozen, and consumers should know that lingcod meat often appears with a green hue. Do not mistake this for a spoiled fish. Unlike other white-meat fish, lingcod is unique in that its meat appears green when raw but finishes white when cooked. It's also best to choose smaller-size lingcod, as the giants (40 pounds and over) are not as savory.

Achieving a lifelong ambition, Chef Christine Keff opened Flying Fish in July of 1995 after stints at several top restaurants on both coasts. Flying Fish appeared in major publications across the country including the *New York Times, Bon Appetit, Gourmet, Wine Spectator, Decanter,* and *Food and Wine.* In March of 1999, it received a 4-star rating by the *Seattle Post-Intelligencer*, sharing this award with only one other restaurant in the city. Two months later, the James Beard Foundation recognized Chef Keff as the "Best Chef in the Pacific Northwest/Hawaii." In 2003 Chef Keff was featured in a lengthy interview on NPR, in addition to features on CNN's "On the Menu" and the Food Network's *Dining Around*. Her powerful relationships with regional fishermen, as well as her use of global spices and local and sustainable ingredients (including certified naturally grown produce from her own subsidized farm) to create signature dishes, continue to bring her national attention as Seattle's seafood expert. ✑

"Alaska's well-managed fisheries make serving sustainably harvested seafood quite easy. For the most part, if you buy Alaskan, you know you have purchased a sustainably harvested fish. It's an easy way to make your contribution to a sustainable planet."

Lingcod Tacos

HOW TO MAKE THE TACOS: In a mixing bowl, combine the paprika, cumin, oregano, chipotle flakes, black and white pepper, ground chili, garlic salt, and salt, and mix thoroughly.

Cut the fish into 2-inch cubes. Sprinkle the lingcod with enough spice mixture to thoroughly coat the fish. In a large (12 inches or larger) sauté pan, heat enough oil to coat the bottom of the pan. When the oil is hot, add ¼ of the fish cubes. Toss, browning on all sides, until the fish begins to flake. Transfer to a sheet pan and keep warm in a 150°F oven. Repeat the process with the rest of the fish, ¼ at a time.

HOW TO PLATE: Place the lingcod on a large serving platter, along with guacamole, your favorite salsa, and warm tortillas.

MAKES 6 SERVINGS

1 tablespoon paprika
1 tablespoon cumin
1 teaspoon oregano
1 teaspoon chipotle flakes
½ teaspoon black pepper
¼ teaspoon white pepper
¼ teaspoon ground pequin chili
1 teaspoon garlic salt
1 tablespoon salt
2 pounds fresh Alaskan lingcod
Vegetable oil, for searing
Fresh guacamole
Fresh salsa
Warm tortillas (flour or corn)

"One of the best and easiest ways to cook lingcod is by baking. The fish does very well in the oven, either with a vegetable-based sauce or a bread crumb mix with a little fat of some kind."

Lingcod with Smoked Tomato Vinaigrette and Spring Vegetables

For the Vinaigrette
2 Roma tomatoes
1 tablespoon tomato paste
1 teaspoon chopped shallot
¼ cup sherry vinegar
1 cup olive oil
Pinch of salt and pepper, to
taste

For the Vegetables
12 baby carrots, peeled
1 cup shelled peas
6 baby yellow beets, peeled
6 baby turnips, peeled
6 fingerling potatoes
1 tablespoon olive oil
1 clove garlic, smashed
2 sprigs fresh thyme
Pinch salt and pepper, to
taste

For the Lingcod
2 tablespoons canola oil
4 6-ounce pieces fresh
Alaskan lingcod, 1 to 2
inches thick
2 tablespoons butter
Pinch salt and pepper, to
taste

Note: This dish is great in the spring when the vegetables are small and tender. Use any vegetables you like. The vegetables listed below are just an example.

HOW TO SMOKE THE ROMA TOMATOES: It's easy to smoke vegetables in a small home smoker, like a Smokey Joe. Treat the tomatoes like anything else you'd smoke—decide how much smoke taste you want. For this recipe, you want a medium smoky flavor, enough to have it come through in the vinaigrette, without tasting only smoke. Because smokers vary so much, a little trial and error is often the case when deciding exactly how long to leave the tomatoes in.

HOW TO MAKE THE VINAIGRETTE: Puree the tomatoes, paste, shallot, and vinegar in a blender until smooth. With the blender running, slowly add the oil in a steady stream. Season with salt and pepper and reserve.

HOW TO MAKE THE VEGETABLES: Blanche the vegetables (except the potatoes) in boiling, salted water until al dente. You'll probably have to boil each vegetable separately, as they will vary in size. When blanched, chill the vegetables in cold water, drain, and set aside.

Next, roast the fingerling potatoes in a 350°F oven after tossing them with the olive oil, garlic, and thyme sprigs. Roast until they yield to a knife inserted into the flesh. Season with salt and pepper to taste.

How to make the lingcod: Heat the canola oil in a sauté pan large enough to hold all the fish. When the oil is shimmering, add the fish and cook on medium until the pieces can be lifted off the bottom. Turn the fish over and finish cooking, until the fish flakes.

While the fish is cooking, heat the 2 tablespoons of butter in a sauté pan and add the vegetables and potatoes. Heat through and season with salt and pepper.

How to plate: Divide the vegetables between four plates and place a piece of lingcod on top. Drizzle with the vinaigrette and serve.

MAKES 4 SERVINGS

Lingcod in Kasu Marinade

HOW TO MAKE THE MARINADE: Blend the kasu lees, soy sauce, Mirin, sake, and water to a smooth paste. Coat the lingcod and marinate for 2 hours.

HOW TO MAKE THE BROTH: Combine the chicken stock, soy sauce, dashi powder, preserved lemon, mirin, and sake in a small saucepan. Bring to a boil, turn the heat down, and simmer for 5 minutes. Season with salt.

HOW TO MAKE THE LINGCOD: Heat the canola oil in a sauté pan large enough to hold the 4 pieces of fish. When the oil is shimmering, add the fish. Cook over medium heat until the fish will lift away from the pan. Turn the pieces over and finish cooking, until the fish flakes.

HOW TO PLATE: Divide the lingcod in shallow bowls, such as soup plates, ladle the broth around the fish, and serve with steamed baby bok choy.

MAKES 4 SERVINGS

For the Marinade
¼ cup kasu lees (alternative: light mayo and lemon pepper)
1 tablespoon soy sauce
1 tablespoon mirin (sweet cooking wine)
1 tablespoon sake
2 tablespoons water
4 6-ounce pieces fresh Alaskan lingcod, 1 to 2 inches thick

For the Broth
1 cup chicken stock
1 tablespoon soy sauce
1 teaspoon dashi-no-moto powder (available at Asian markets)
1 teaspoon diced preserved lemon
1 teaspoon mirin
1 cup sake
Pinch salt, to taste

For the Lingcod
2 tablespooons canola oil
4 baby bok choy, steamed (optional)

"When pan-searing, it's important to get your oil heated to the point that it shimmers before adding the fish so it doesn't stick. Again, the lingcod's low fat content makes this a necessity."

Alaskan Seafood Stifado

½ cup olive oil
3 bay leaves
3 cloves
1 pound pearl onions, peeled
2 cloves garlic
1 pound garden tomatoes,
    peeled and pureed
½ cup red wine
6 ounces fresh Alaskan
    lingcod
10 Pacific blue mussels
10 Alaska littleneck clams
½ pound fresh Alaskan spot
    prawns
1 tablespoon chopped fresh
    parsley
4 tablespoons chopped fresh
    fennel fronds
2 tablespoons white wine
    vinegar
Pinch salt and black pepper,
    to taste

HOW TO MAKE THE SEAFOOD STIFADO: Heat the olive oil in a large, shallow pan and add the bay leaves and cloves. Heat just until you can smell the cloves, then add the onions and garlic. Cook slowly on medium heat until the vegetables are softened and slightly browned, about 20 minutes.

Add the fresh tomato puree and red wine. Simmer until the tomato thickens, about 20 minutes. Cut the lingcod into 4 small pieces. Lay the fish and the mussels, clams, and prawns on top of the sauce and cover. Simmer gently until the cod has cooked and the mussels and clams have opened. Remove the seafood and transfer to a plate.

Add the parsley, fennel, and vinegar to the sauce. Season with salt and pepper.

HOW TO PLATE: Divide the sauce in the bottom of four large bowls. Divide the seafood and arrange on top. Serve immediately.

MAKES 4 SERVINGS

> "Because of its low fat content, lingcod does not do well on the grill."

"Lingcod are actually not true cods but are of the greenling family. With their oversized heads and muscular, brown- and copper-blotched bodies, this species has been given the scientific name *Ophiodon elongates,* or 'long-toothed snake.' "

Soy-Glazed Lingcod with Ginger Butter Sauce and Eggplant Relish

HOW TO MAKE THE LINGCOD: Combine the soy sauce, sake, sugar, and water, and stir well to combine while dissolving the sugar. Pour over the cod and marinate for 1 hour. Remove the lingcod from the marinade and pat dry. Sauté in a just a little vegetable oil until brown on one side. Flip the fish, turn down the heat, and cook until flaky, about 7 minutes.

HOW TO MAKE THE GINGER BUTTER SAUCE: Place the shallots, ginger, mirin, soy sauce, and vinegar into a saucepan. Bring to a boil and simmer until liquid has evaporated. Add the cream and veal stock. Simmer until reduced by ¾. Remove from the heat, and whisk in the butter piece by piece. When the butter is completely incorporated, strain through a fine strainer.

HOW TO MAKE THE EGGPLANT RELISH: Sweat the garlic, ginger, and shallots in the oil until tender. Add the eggplant and stir well, cooking 3 to 4 minutes. Add the hoisin, vinegar, and mirin. Stir and cover. Allow to simmer for 5 minutes.

HOW TO PLATE: Divide the lingcod among four serving plates and dress the fish with the ginger butter sauce and the hoisin eggplant relish.

MAKES 4 SERVINGS

For the Marinade
¼ cup soy sauce
½ cup sake
2 tablespoons sugar
1 cup water
4 6-ounce portions fresh Alaskan lingcod, 1 to 2 inches thick
1 tablespoon vegetable oil

For the Ginger Butter Sauce
1 shallot, sliced
1 piece fresh ginger, peeled and sliced
¼ cup mirin
2 tablespoons soy sauce
¼ cup rice wine vinegar
¼ cup cream
¼ cup veal stock
¼ pound butter, cut into 1-inch cubes

For the Eggplant Relish
1 teaspoon chopped garlic
1 teaspoon peeled and chopped ginger
1 teaspoon minced shallot
¼ cup canola oil
½ pound Japanese eggplant, small dice (approximately ¼ inch x ¼ inch)
¼ cup hoisin sauce
1 teaspoon rice vinegar
1 teaspoon mirin

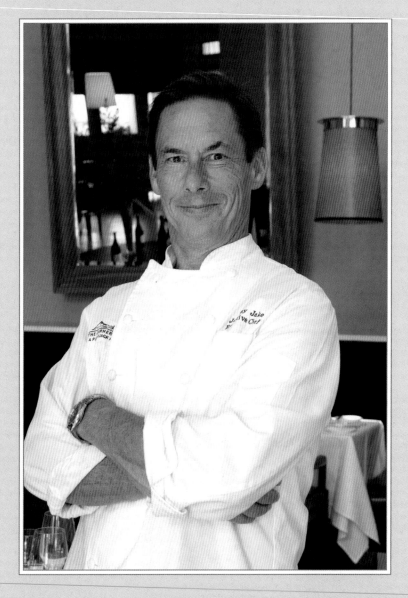

"Sustainable management practices regarding our oceans must be embraced by the world community. Overfishing, pollution, and climate change are all critical challenges to the future of our fisheries. Purchasing from responsible fisheries, vendors, and guest education are the chef's tools in supporting the proper stewardship of our ocean resources."

—Executive Chef Jeffrey Jake

Chapter 8

PACIFIC COD

EXECUTIVE CHEF JEFFREY JAKE—THE CARNEROS INN

*C*od is the king of whitefish, a species over which wars have been fought and from which trading fortunes have been made for hundreds of years. Today, two types of cod—Atlantic and Pacific—are as popular as ever. Their flakey white flesh has almost universal appeal.

Found throughout the North Pacific, the Pacific cod (sometimes called "true cod," "gray cod," or "P-cod") is the world's second-largest whitefish resource. The Alaska fishery is by far the most important Pacific cod fishery, and Alaska fishermen catch between 250,000 and 300,000 tons of Pacific cod each year using longline gear. The rest is caught by trawlers and pot boats.

There can be significant quality differences with Pacific cod, depending upon the time of year the fish is caught, but quality is also a function of how the fish were handled.

In his role as executive chef for The Carneros Inn, Chef Jeffrey Jake is inspired by the abundance of fresh local ingredients that abound in Napa Valley's Carneros wine-growing region. Chef Jake oversees The Carneros Inn's private dining restaurant, the Hilltop Dining Room; the sophisticated wine country restaurant FARM; local favorite The Boon Fly Café; and all catering and room service for the inn. One of his primary responsibilities is managing the seasonally changing menus created primarily from the Carneros region's bountiful array of top-quality produce, cattle ranches, and award-winning cheese producers.

Chef Jake has been the recipient of a number of awards and accolades during his career, including the Conde Nast *Traveler* "Best Resort in North America" award (The Lodge at Pebble Beach), three stars from the *San Francisco Chronicle* (Sonoma Mission Inn), and *Gourmet Magazine*'s "Top Ten Wine Country Restaurants" (Sonoma Mission Inn).

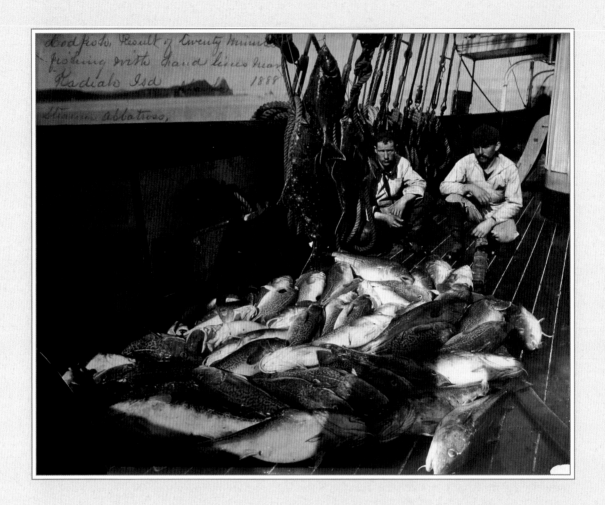

"Cod is a remarkable character with a fascinating history. A look back at the cod also gives us a lesson in fully utilizing our catch from head to tail, and don't forget the curative properties of cod liver oil."

Alaskan Cod Sashimi with Warm Soy-Citrus Infusion

HOW TO MAKE THE SOY-CITRUS SAUCE: Mix together the lemon juice, lime juice, rice vinegar, soy sauce, Mirin, dried bonito flakes, and cayenne, and allow to stand for at least 4 hours at room temperature. Refrigerate until ready to use.

HOW TO MAKE THE COD SASHIMI: Place the cod fillet in the freezer for 20 minutes after removing all the pin bones and dark trim. This will help achieve a very thin cut of cod.

HOW TO PLATE: Remove cod from freezer, slice, and lay 3 ounces of sliced cod slightly overlapping each other on each plate. It is best to place each piece of fish as you go. Over medium heat, warm the soy-citrus sauce along with the fruity olive oil. It should be warm to the touch. You do not want the sauce too hot or it will cook the fish. Sprinkle the cod slices with Asian pear and green onion. Spoon over the warm sauce and finish with the radish and celery leaves.

MAKES 6 SERVINGS

For the Soy-Citrus Sauce
1 cup lemon juice
1/3 cup lime juice
1/4 cup rice vinegar
1 cup soy sauce
1/4 cup Mirin
1/2 cup dried bonito flakes
Pinch cayenne

For the Cod Sashimi
18 ounces Alaskan cod, cut paper thin
1 1/2 cups soy-citrus sauce
2 tablespoons fruity olive oil
1/4 cup small-diced Asian pear
1/4 cup thin-sliced green onion
1/2 cup thin-sliced radish
1/2 cup young celery leaves

"I spent a good portion of my career working in the Monterey Bay area, which enabled me to source fresh seafood from well-known vendors. One such day in my first executive chef position at the Old Bathhouse Restaurant, a gentleman came to my back door with cooler in tow. He asked if I would like to purchase a cod he'd just got his hands on. It was very exciting, and as we opened the top of the cooler to inspect his fish, the cod flopped out of the cooler. I think I broke the Olympic long jump record as that happened. We both broke out laughing and, of course, I purchased the fish."

Alaskan Cod and Toasted Curry Cake
with Blood Orange and Belgian Endive Slaw

For the Steamed Cod

2 shallots, peeled and cut in half

3 sprigs fresh thyme

6 black peppercorns

1 bay leaf

½ cup white wine (sauvignon blanc) or water

1 pound cleaned cod meat, cut into 2-inch pieces

For the Cod and Curry Cake

1 tablespoon curry

¼ cup fresh squeezed lemon juice

¼ cup sour cream

¼ cup mayonnaise

¼ cup small-diced green apple

2 tablespoons small-diced chives

¼ cup panko, and more for dusting

Pinch salt and white pepper, to taste

4 tablespoons grapeseed oil

For the Blood Orange and Belgian Endive Slaw

1 red Belgian endive

2 blood oranges

2 tablespoons blood orange juice

1 tablespoon rice vinegar

Pinch salt and black pepper, to taste

2 tablespoons toasted coconut

How to steam the cod: Place the shallots, thyme, black peppercorn, bay leaf, and wine into a large saucepan and bring to a boil. When boiling, add the cod and cover. Reduce heat and cook for 5 to 8 minutes, until cod is cooked through. Remove fish and drain on paper towels, pressing to remove liquid from the fish. Allow to cool completely.

How to make the cod and curry cake: Crumble the steamed cod into small pieces. Next, lightly toast the curry on the stovetop in a nonstick pan to release essential oils and intensify aroma profiles. In a bowl, mix the cod with the curry, along with the lemon juice, sour cream, mayonnaise, green apple, chives, panko, salt, and pepper. Work gently to combine, and refrigerate for at least 1 hour.

After chilling, form 2-ounce patties, and lightly coat each one in panko. In a nonstick skillet over medium-high heat, heat 2 tablespoons of grapeseed oil and cook half the cod cakes 3 to 4 minutes per side. Remove and plate. Discard the used oil, then heat the remaining 2 tablespoons of oil and cook the remaining cakes.

How to make the blood orange and Belgian endive slaw: Separate the endive into leaves. Wash and dry the leaves completely. Lengthwise cut them julienne-style. Segment the blood oranges, removing all of the membrane. Cut them in thirds. Toss the endive and orange segments together and gently dress with the blood orange juice and rice vinegar. Season with salt and pepper.

How to plate: Place 2 cod cakes on each plate. Place 2 tablespoons of slaw on the cod cakes and sprinkle with toasted coconut.

MAKES 8 SERVINGS

Alaskan Cod and Saffron Butter Wrapped in Grape Leaves with Parsnip Puree and Lemon Crème Fraiche

For the Alaskan Cod
8 4-ounce pieces Alaskan cod
Pinch salt and pepper, to taste
½ cup grapeseed oil, for searing fish
8–16 grape leaves
½ cup olive oil, for grape leaves
8 tablespoons compound butter

For the Parsnip Puree
2–3 parsnips
1 cup heavy cream
¼ cup water
Pinch salt
1 tablespoon unsalted butter

For the Saffron Butter
½ pound soft unsalted butter
1 pinch saffron threads, bloomed in 1 ounce water
2 teaspoons small-cut chives
2 teaspoons minced shallots
1 teaspoon fresh grated ginger
2 teaspoons salt

For the Lemon Crème Fraiche
4 lemons
4 tablespoons kosher salt
1 cup fresh lemon juice
¼ cinnamon stick
1 whole clove
2 cups crème fraiche

HOW TO MAKE THE COD: Season the cod with salt and pepper, and heat the grapeseed oil in a sauté pan. Sear the cod over medium-high heat 2 to 3 minutes, depending on the thickness of the cod fillet. Remove and cool.

Wash the grape leaves and dry with paper towels. Rub the leaves with olive oil and place the leaves on a flat surface. Place one piece of cod on one or two leaves. Place a tablespoon of butter on top of each cod piece and wrap the grape leaves, securing with a toothpick, if needed. Place the cod wrapped in grape leaves on a roasting rack and into a preheated 375°F oven for 8 to 10 minutes. Test for doneness and remove to a warm place for plating.

HOW TO MAKE THE PARSNIP PUREE: Cut the parsnips into ½-inch pieces. Place in a saucepan with the cream, water, and salt. Bring to a boil and simmer about 20 minutes. Strain the parsnips and reserve the cream. Puree the parsnips, adding butter and enough cream for a thick but creamy puree. Add more salt to taste if desired.

HOW TO MAKE THE SAFFRON BUTTER: Place the butter, saffron threads, chives, shallots, ginger, and salt in a mixer with paddle attachment. Blend until smooth and refrigerate until ready to use.

HOW TO MAKE THE LEMON CRÈME FRAICHE: Preheat oven to 200°F. Wash the lemons and cut off both ends. Cut into quarters. In a small roasting pan, combine the lemons, salt, cinnamon stick and clove. Add enough lemon juice to cover the lemons. Cover the roasting pan and cook approximately 3 hours. Remove the cinnamon stick and clove, reserving the poaching liquid. Refrigerate the lemons until chilled. Remove and discard the lemon fruit remaining on the skin and julienne the lemon skin.

How to plate: Place a tablespoon or two of parsnip puree in the middle of individual serving bowls. Remove toothpicks (if used) and place the grape leaf–wrapped fish on the puree. Spoon a little of the lemon poaching liquid around the plate. Serve with a small sauce-boat of crème fraiche topped with the preserved lemon julienne.

MAKES 8 SERVINGS

"Alaskan cod—a cousin to the Atlantic cod—lends itself to many cooking techniques because of its moist and flaky characteristics. The cod's mild flavor profile coupled with a given cooking method allows the cod flavor affinities to pair with a diverse group of supporting ingredients. The cod is also rich in nutrients and low in calories, placing it high on the list as a healthy food choice."

Alaskan Cod Po'boy with Nonnie Bennett's Slaw

For the Cod Po'boy
1 cup canola oil
1 cup cornmeal
1 cup flour
1 teaspoon dried thyme
1 teaspoon cayenne pepper
Pinch salt, to taste
6 5-ounce pieces Alaskan
  cod
1 cup milk

For Nonnie Bennett's Slaw Dressing
2 eggs
3 tablespoons sugar
1 tablespoon flour
3 teaspoons salt
1½ teaspoons dry mustard
¼ teaspoon cayenne
½ cup apple cider vinegar
1 cup milk
1 cup sour cream

For the Slaw Mixture
4 cups shredded cabbage (2
  red and 2 green)
¼ cup thinly sliced red onion
¼ cup shredded fennel
¼ cup thinly sliced cucumber
¼ cup shredded carrot
¼ cup chopped parsley
4 strips crisp bacon,
  crumbled (optional)
6 Kaiser rolls

HOW TO MAKE THE COD PO'BOY: Heat the canola oil in a large skillet over medium heat. Mix together the cornmeal, flour, thyme, cayenne pepper, and salt for dredging on a large plate. Dip the cod in the milk and then lightly but evenly coat the fillets. Make sure the oil is not smoking and place the cod into the hot oil, giving the pieces enough room so they don't touch each other while cooking. Cook 4 to 5 minutes until golden brown. Remove and drain on paper towels.

HOW TO MAKE THE SLAW: Beat the eggs in a stainless steel bowl and place over gently boiling water (or use a double boiler). Add the sugar, flour, salt, mustard, and cayenne, and incorporate. Then add the vinegar, and slowly add the milk. Cook to a custard stage, approximately 15 minutes, and shock in an ice bath to stop the cooking process. When cool, fold in the sour cream. This yields approximately 3 cups. Combine the cabbage, onion, fennel, cucumber, carrot, parsley, and bacon; toss the slaw mixture with enough dressing to evenly coat. Check the seasoning before serving.

HOW TO PLATE: Toast the Kaiser rolls and divide the cod on the rolls. Top with the slaw and serve.

MAKES 6 SERVINGS

Barbecue Alaskan Cod with Summer Vegetables and Olive Oil Crushed Potatoes

For the Alaskan Cod
8 7-ounce fillets fresh
    Alaskan cod, 1¼ inch thick,
    with skin on
½ cup extra-virgin olive oil
Pinch sea salt and fresh
    ground white pepper

For the Olive Oil Crushed Potatoes
2 pounds fingerling potatoes,
    cleaned
½ cup extra-virgin olive oil
¼ cup dry white wine
3 tablespoons sea salt

For the Summer Vegetables
3 ears fresh white corn,
    shucked
1 quart heirloom teardrop
    tomatoes, halved
1 quart fresh arugula
¼ cup fresh parsley leaves
⅓ cup whole fresh tarragon
    leaves
⅓ cup snipped fresh chives
¼ cup torn fresh mint leaves
⅓ cup snap pea flowers
½ cup extra-virgin olive oil
    (lemon EVOO preferred)
Pinch sea salt and fresh
    ground pepper, to taste

HOW TO MAKE THE BARBECUE COD: Prepare an outdoor barbecue or indoor grill on high heat (note: grill is ready when coals burn white). While grill is heating, make three slashes just through the skin of the cod at a slight angle with a sharp kitchen knife. This will prevent the skin from curling the fish and allow the penetration of salt and pepper. Next, rub each cod fillet with olive oil and then evenly salt and pepper each side of fish. Allow at least 15 minutes before grilling. Oil the grill and place the fish skin side down. Cook for 3 to 4 minutes, or until skin is crisp. Turn once and grill other side for 2 to 3 minutes. Remove to a warm platter for plating.

HOW TO MAKE THE OLIVE OIL CRUSHED POTATOES: Preheat the oven to 375°F. Split the fingerling potatoes lengthwise and toss with oil, wine, and salt. Place the potatoes in a baking dish and cover tightly. Cook in the oven for 30 minutes, or until potatoes are tender. Lightly crush the potatoes with the tongs of a fork. Add more olive oil and salt if necessary. (Note: The potatoes can also be baked in foil packages over the grill.)

HOW TO MAKE THE SUMMER VEGETABLES: In a salad bowl, cut the corn off the cobs and press the corn milk from the cobs into the bowl with the back of the knife. Add the tomatoes, arugula, parsley, tarragon, chives, mint, and snap pea flowers to the corn mixture. Drizzle with the olive oil and gently toss. Season with salt and pepper and serve immediately.

"Depending on the thickness of your cod fillet, season the fish evenly 10 to 30 minutes before cooking."

How to plate: On two large platters, place 4 servings of the olive oil crushed potatoes. Bank the cod fillets skin side up next to the potatoes. Top each fillet with a generous portion of the herb and vegetable salad. Drizzle the olive oil and corn milk left in the bowl around the fish. Serve immediately.

MAKES 8 SERVINGS

"The Alaskan halibut fishery has been managed by the International Pacific Halibut Commission since 1923, which is probably why we still have sustainable levels of halibut in our oceans today."

—Executive Chef Paul Buchanan

Chapter 9

PACIFIC HALIBUT

EXECUTIVE CHEF PAUL BUCHANAN—PRIMAL ALCHEMY CATERING

*H*alibut are the largest of all flatfish. Pacific halibut can grow to more than 8 feet long and more than 500 pounds, rightfully earning their Latin name, *Hippoglossus*, or "hippos of the sea."

Alaska halibut are caught by longline, which are typically quarter-mile "skates" of gear with baited hooks strung every 5 to 10 feet. Alaska accounts for approximately 80 percent of the North American harvest of Pacific halibut. The annual quota now averages about 25,000 tons.

Fishing for Pacific halibut is regulated by the International Pacific Halibut Commission. Members from the United States and Canada meet yearly to review research, check the progress of the commercial fishery, and make regulations for the next fishing season. The man-

> **"I love halibut because it's so** versatile and can be created into so many different styled dishes. Halibut can be stuffed with Mediterranean ingredients, pairs well with citrus, can be grilled, and halibut will take to most any spice you throw at it."

agement of halibut fishing by this commission is intended to allow a maximum sustained yield of halibut.

The term "primal alchemy" describes humankind's first attempt to turn raw meats and vegetables into rich, flavorful dishes. Chef Paul Buchanan expertly applies this alchemy with today's technology to create exceptional cuisine bursting with flavor for his Primal Alchemy Catering.

Chef Buchanan has set himself apart from the many caterers in Southern California through his passion for using sustainable, organic foods. He has achieved a great respect and natural flair for vegetarian cooking, in addition to his ease with omnivore menus. In conjunction with incredibly fresh, seasonal components, Chef Buchanan encourages his clients to plan the fare. He does not offer rote meals; rather, he customizes each menu, working with both his client's needs and the seasonal offerings. ❧

Herb-Marinated Halibut Brochettes with Meyer Lemon Oil

For the Marinade
1 20-ounce Alaskan halibut fillet, cut into 24 1-inch square cubes
3 tablespoons olive oil
3 tablespoons canola oil
1 teaspoon finely chopped fresh thyme leaves
1 teaspoon fresh very finely chopped rosemary leaves
1 teaspoon very finely chopped garlic
¼ teaspoon kosher salt
2 pinches ground white pepper

For the Meyer Lemon Oil
2 Meyer lemons, zest of the skin, yellow only, no white
1 cup canola oil

For the Halibut Brochettes
8 metal brochette skewers (or 10- to 12-inch bamboo skewers, soaked in water)
2–3 Meyer lemons, cut into quarters lengthwise, then into ½-inch wedges
24 multicolored heirloom cherry tomatoes

HOW TO MAKE THE HALIBUT MARINADE: Keep the halibut cubes cold while you mix the olive oil, canola oil, thyme, rosemary, garlic, salt, and pepper in a stainless steel bowl (the marinade). Add the halibut to the marinade and refrigerate for 30 to 60 minutes.

HOW TO MAKE THE MEYER LEMON OIL: Place the Meyer lemon zest and canola oil in a small pot over low heat. Do not boil, but when the zest sizzles, remove from heat and let the oil sit for about 2 hours. Strain the oil and reserve. For stronger lemon flavor, the oil can set out for up to 24 hours before straining.

HOW TO MAKE THE HALIBUT BROCHETTES: Using 12-inch skewers, alternate placing the lemon wedges, marinated halibut cubes, and cherry tomatoes on the skewers. There should be 3 pieces of each per skewer. Using a charcoal or gas grill heated to high, cook the skewers. (Note: Make sure the grill has been cleaned with a wire brush and the grates of the grill are oiled just before adding the skewers.) Position the skewers on the grill pointing to the upper left corner (10 o'clock). After about 1 minute, you should have a good grill mark, so move the skewers so the tips are pointing to the upper right (2 o'clock). Cook about 1 more minute then flip skewers over and repeat on the other side. Do not burn or overcook, but do not eat halibut that is raw. The skewers will be ready to serve immediately.

HOW TO PLATE: Serve the skewers over a mixed green salad with avocado and manchego cheese, or over red cargo rice. Before serving, season the skewers with salt, white pepper, and a drizzle of the Meyer lemon oil.

MAKES 4 SERVINGS

Grilled Halibut with Pancetta, Onion, Morels, and Kabocha Pumpkin

1 medium kabocha pumpkin, cut in half, seeds removed
3 cups water (reserve 1½ cups pumpkin water)
2 tablespoons heavy whipping cream
¾ teaspoon kosher salt
Pinch ground white pepper
¼ teaspoon Chinese 5 spice
5 ounces pancetta, cut into lardons (¼ inch x ¼ inch x ½ inch)
3 medium cippolini onions, peeled, cut in half, and sliced
3 ounces dry morel mushrooms, small caps, rehydrated in warm water, cut in half
1 teaspoon finely cut fresh sage
1 24-ounce Alaskan halibut fillet, cut into 4 6-ounce portions
1 tablespoon canola oil
Pinch kosher salt, to taste
Pinch ground white pepper, to taste

HOW TO MAKE THE PUMPKIN: Preheat oven to 450°F. Place pumpkin halves on a sheet pan with about 3 cups of water. Roast the pumpkin for about 20 minutes, or until soft. Remove from oven, let pumpkin cool slightly, then use a spoon to scrape all the meat from the skins and place it into a blender. You should get about 2 cups of pumpkin meat. Scrape any of the caramelized bits from the pan and mix with the water. Add the cream, salt, white pepper, and Chinese 5 spice, and blend until smooth. Adjust the flavor and consistency and strain the puree to remove any chunks. Set aside.

HOW TO MAKE THE PANCETTA, ONION, AND MOREL MUSHROOMS: Place the pancetta on a pan in a 300°F oven for about 10 minutes until it has browned and rendered some of its fat. Remove the pancetta and reserve the excess fat to sauté the onion. Next, sauté the onion over medium heat in the same pan. Cook the onion until translucent and slightly browned. Add the morel mushrooms and cook for at least 1 minute. Add the pancetta back to the pan, along with the sage. Continue cooking for about 1 minute, then adjust the seasoning if necessary. This is the topping that will be placed over the fish.

HOW TO MAKE THE HALIBUT: Heat a gas or charcoal grill on high. Coat the fillets with a thin brushing of canola oil and season them with kosher salt and ground white pepper. When the grill is hot (note: make sure the grates are brushed clean and oiled), place the

> "Remember that portions that are to be cooked at the same time should be cut the same size and thickness to ensure even cooking."

halibut on the grill, presentation side down, pointing to the upper left corner (10 o'clock). After about 2 minutes or so, you should have a good grill mark, so move the fish so the tip is pointing to the upper right (2 o'clock); cook about 2 more minutes, then flip the fish over and repeat on the other side. Depending on how thick your fish fillet is, you may need to place the fish into a 300°F oven until it is finished (cooked through but moist).

How to plate: Place the warm pumpkin puree on the bottom of four warm plates, and place the halibut on the puree. Top the fish with the sautéed pancetta, onion, and mushroom ragu, and serve immediately.

MAKES 4 SERVINGS

Oven-Roasted Pacific Halibut with Citrus Panade and Seafood Cream Sauce

For the Seafood Cream Sauce
2 live Alaska littleneck clams
2 live Pacific blue mussels
2 Alaska shrimp, shells on
2 fresh thyme sprigs
2 cups dry white wine
3 cups heavy whipping cream
Kosher salt and ground white pepper, to taste

For the Citrus Panade
6 ounces butter, unsalted and soft
5 ounces bread crumbs
5 ounces pistachio nuts, roasted and chopped
2 teaspoons finely chopped fresh Italian parsley
1 orange, zested, no white, chopped finely
1 teaspoon kosher salt
$\frac{1}{4}$ teaspoon finely ground white pepper

HOW TO MAKE THE SEAFOOD CREAM SAUCE: Begin the sauce by placing the clams, mussels, shrimp, thyme, and wine into a nonreactive pot (stainless steel is best). Reduce the wine over medium heat until $\frac{1}{4}$ to $\frac{1}{2}$ cup of liquid left. Add the cream and reduce volume to 2 cups. The sauce will be thick at this point. Strain the sauce into a stainless steel bowl that you can cover and keep warm until ready to plate. (Note: Make sure to taste the sauce and adjust the seasoning with kosher salt and white pepper.)

HOW TO MAKE THE CITRUS PANADE: In a bowl, mix the softened butter, bread crumbs, pistachio nuts, parsley, orange zest, and salt and white pepper with a rubber spatula until creamy.

"While working one day as a young line cook with very little experience, I once served halibut to a guest who had ordered the white seabass from the menu. I remember grabbing the wrong fish from the refrigerator and was terrified my mistake would be noticed. Later, the waiter of that table came to me directly at the end of the meal and told me the guest had boasted how wonderful the fish was—the best seafood they had ever eaten. I was relieved, and two restaurant jobs later, I found myself at the Water Grill in downtown Los Angeles, learning more about seafood than I had ever known before."

How to make the halibut: Season both sides of the halibut fillets with kosher salt and white pepper. Place the seasoned fillets on a cookie sheet that has been coated with canola oil. Use a metal cake spatula to spread a ¼-inch layer of citrus panade evenly onto the top of each piece of halibut. Refrigerate fish for at least 30 minutes. When ready to cook the fish, place the cookie sheet into a 425°F oven and check for doneness after 10 minutes. The halibut is done when it reaches 145°F at the center or when you can easily push a knife through the flesh with no resistance. The citrus panade crust should also be golden to medium brown.

How to make the quinoa: Simply follow the quinoa package directions. When the quinoa is finished cooking, add the diced tomato, chives, salt, and pepper, mix, and keep warm and covered. A sprinkling of good quality avocado, walnut, or other nut oil will enhance the finished quinoa.

How to plate: Divide the quinoa among the centers of four plates. Place a halibut fillet on top, and ladle some of the warm seafood cream sauce over the fish and around the quinoa in a circular fashion. Garnish with chopped chives and citrus zest.

MAKES 4 SERVINGS

For the Halibut
4 6-ounce fillets fresh Alaska halibut, approximately 1½ inches thick
Kosher salt and ground white pepper, to taste
Canola oil, as needed to grease baking pan

For the Quinoa
3 cups quinoa, prepared according to package directions
¾ cup diced fresh tomato, drained of any liquid
1 tablespoon fresh chopped chives, reserving some for garnish
Kosher salt and ground white pepper, to taste
2 tablespoons citrus zest threads (orange and lemon), blanched once or twice in boiling water then shocked in cold water and dried on paper towels, for garnish

"After tasting the fish I have cooked, many people ask what I did to the fish to make it taste so delicious. All I use is salt and pepper to season fish. Seasoning food correctly is the single most important talent of any cook."

Potlatch Cedar-Planked Halibut with Apple Cider Gastrique

For the Halibut Brine
2 ounces kosher salt
2 ounces sugar
5 cups warm water
1/4 teaspoon ground black pepper
1/4 teaspoon dry, granulated garlic
2 bay leaves
1/4 teaspoon dry, ground ginger
1/4 teaspoon dry, ground mace
1/4 teaspoon ground nutmeg
1/2 teaspoon chopped fresh thyme
1/2 teaspoon chopped fresh tarragon
1/2 teaspoon chopped fresh marjoram
1 24-ounce Alaskan halibut fillet, cut into 4 6-ounce portions

For the Gastrique
2 cups apple cider
1 cup apple cider vinegar
1 cup sugar
1 stick cinnamon
1 star anise
1/4 teaspoon kosher salt

For the Halibut
Untreated cedar plank, any size that will fit in your oven
Heirloom carrots, steamed until just tender
Pink peppercorns (optional)

HOW TO MAKE THE BRINE: At least a day ahead, make the brine by mixing together the salt, sugar, warm water, black pepper, garlic, bay leaves, ginger, mace, nutmeg, thyme, tarragon, and marjoram. Wisk until the salt and sugar are dissolved. Let the brine cool before submerging the fish. When cool, add the halibut and store covered in the refrigerator for 4 to 6 hours. For larger whole sides of fish, the marinating time can be 8 to 12 hours.

HOW TO MAKE THE GASTRIQUE: Add the apple cider, apple cider vinegar, sugar, cinnamon stick, star anise, and salt into a nonreactive pan. Bring to a boil and reduce until the sauce is the thickness of warm honey. Taste and adjust the flavor so it is balanced. Pass the sauce through a fine strainer and let cool. Once cool, it can be placed into a squeeze bottle, labeled, and stored in the refrigerator until needed. Bring gastrique to room temperature before using to sauce the fish.

HOW TO MAKE THE HALIBUT: Remove the fish from brine, and rinse under cool water. Pat the fish dry with paper towels. Next, place the fish into a smoker for about 10 to 15 minutes. It's best to place a pan of ice under the rack where the fish is being smoked to prevent the fish from being cooked by the heat of the smoker. (Use an electric smoker set at 180°F.) Remove the fish and place into the refrigerator to cool. Before serving, place the smoked halibut onto a cedar plank and place into a 300°F oven until the internal fish temperature is about 145°F (use a digital thermometer).

HOW TO PLATE: While the fish is baking, steam the carrots or other local seasonal root vegetables until just tender. Remove the plank from the oven when the fish is done, drizzle the fish with the apple cider gastrique, and sprinkle with pink peppercorns.

MAKES 4 SERVINGS

"Many people don't know how to buy fish and are afraid to ask the right questions. It's best to buy fish from a reputable source. Always ask questions about where a particular fish comes from, fresh or frozen, wild or farmed, and ask to smell the fish. Fresh fish doesn't smell much, but may have a faint smell of the ocean. If you learn how to buy whole fish, you'll have a better chance of evaluating the freshness. Always look for clear eyes, fresh ocean smell at the gills, and a resilient flesh that bounces back to the touch."

Imu-Style Steamed Halibut, Red Cargo Rice, and Huckleberries

HOW TO MAKE THE RED CARGO RICE: In a large saucepan, add the rice, water, and pinch of sea salt. (Note: Soak your rice 30 minutes before cooking if you like a softer consistency.) Once the water and rice come to a boil, reduce the heat, cover, and simmer until the water is absorbed, about 20 minutes. When the rice is done, fluff with a fork and sprinkle with the avocado oil, season again with salt, and fold in the chopped hazelnuts.

HOW TO MAKE THE HALIBUT: Season the halibut portions with sea salt on both sides. Lay a base of seaweed (or leek tops) on the bottom of a steamer (note: a bamboo steamer over a pot of simmering water is the best method, but a stainless-steel steamer will work too). Place the fish on top of the seaweed, and cover the fish with more seaweed. Cooking time may vary from 10 to 15 minutes, depending on the thickness of the fish. Ultimately, you want the fish to reach 145°F in the center, so use a digital thermometer for an accurate reading.

HOW TO MAKE THE SPINACH: Using a large sauté pan over medium-high heat, add the oil, butter, and garlic. Stir the garlic and cook until fragrant (do not burn). Add the spinach leaves and keep the mixture moving until the spinach collapses. Season with salt and pepper and cook no longer than 1 minute.

HOW TO PLATE: Place a bed of sautéed spinach on a warm plate. Remove fish from steamer and place centered on top of spinach. Sprinkle huckleberries and some of their juice over the top of the fish. A pinch of Alea Red Clay Salt or other good quality sea salt is a nice finish to this dish just before serving.

MAKES 4 SERVINGS

For the Red Cargo Rice
2 cups red cargo rice (available at most Asian markets)
3 cups water
Pinch sea salt
2 tablespoons avocado oil (or walnut or hazelnut oil)
$1/2$ cup toasted chopped hazelnuts

For the Halibut
$1^1/_2$ pounds fresh Alaska halibut fillets, cut into 4- to 6-ounce portions
Pinch sea salt, to taste
$1^1/_2$ pounds fresh seaweed (or leek tops)

For the Spinach
1 tablespoon canola oil
1 tablespoon butter
3 cloves garlic, sliced thin
1 pound fresh spinach, stems removed
Pinch kosher salt and ground white pepper, to taste
$1/2$ cup huckleberries (fresh or frozen)

"Because great taste is the very foundation of my cooking, starting with the freshest, most flavorful ingredients is imperative. When buying for my restaurants or my home, I want to know where everything comes from and how it was raised or grown. I believe we need to reconnect with the land and the food chain because the buying decisions we make do have an impact and effect on our world. Overfishing, pollution, and heavy metals in some of our fish populations are unfortunate realities. As a responsible citizen of the world, I want to do my part to help resolve these issues rather than contribute to their spread. I hope my beliefs and the choices I make in acting in accordance with them will resonate with people and prompt them to think about the many options that exist when it comes to choosing food."

—Executive Chef Cal Stamenov

Chapter 10

PACIFIC HALIBUT CHEEKS

EXECUTIVE CHEF CAL STAMENOV—BERNARDUS LODGE

*H*alibut cheeks are rounded sections of succulent meat extracted from the head area. The white meat is mildly sweet, but unlike the firm, flaky meat found in the body, halibut cheeks are uniquely textured yet extremely tender. Because halibut cheeks are not always available, they can be pricey when they hit the market. Commonly the size of large scallops, halibut cheeks are considered a delicacy and are very versatile in the kitchen because they can be baked, broiled, pan-fried, or poached.

Chef Cal Stamenov has created an innovative culinary concept for Bernardus Lodge featuring California country cuisine in the main dining room, Marinus at Bernardus Lodge. Wickets, the bar and bistro, features bistro-style cuisine in a light and casual setting.

As a graduate of the California Culinary Academy, Chef Stamenov, who is steeped in the European tradition of culinary artistry, has found the Central Coast provides him access to an inspiring range of ingredients whose essence and flavor is appreciable in every bite. These come to him by way of the relationships he has forged with growers, fishermen, and foragers. Chef Stamenov also has his own organic herb and vegetable gardens and vineyards at Bernardus Lodge. With a treasure trove of impeccable products, Chef Stamenov is able to cook with the seasons and rarely has to look further than his own backyard for inspiration.

Halibut Cheek "Wellington" with Fennel Sauce, Organic Greens, and Hazelnut Vinaigrette

For the Hazelnut Vinaigrette
1 tablespoon olive oil
1/2 tablespoon dijon mustard
1/4 cup hazelnut oil
2 tablespoons sherry vinegar
1/4 cup red wine vinegar
1/2 cup vegetable oil
Pinch salt and pepper, to taste

For the Fennel Sauce
2 bulbs fennel, finely sliced
1 tablespoon extra-virgin olive oil
1/4 cup sauvignon blanc
1 tablespoon butter
Pinch salt and pepper, to taste

For the Mushroom Duxelle
1 tablespoon olive oil
2 cloves garlic, thinly sliced
2 cups wild mushrooms (porcini recommended)
2 sprigs fresh thyme
Salt and pepper, to taste

For the Halibut Cheeks
1 sheet puff pastry
4 ounces foie gras
4 halibut cheeks
1 black truffle, sliced (optional)
1 egg, whisked
1 tablespoon water
8 ounces organic mixed greens

HOW TO MAKE THE HAZELNUT VINAIGRETTE: Combine the olive oil, dijon mustard, hazelnut oil, sherry vinegar, and red wine vinegar. Whisk in the vegetable oil. Season with salt and pepper.

HOW TO MAKE THE FENNEL SAUCE: In a hot pan, sweat the fennel and olive oil for 4 to 5 minutes (or until fennel is tender) on low heat. Add the sauvignon blanc and cook for an additional 3 minutes. Transfer to a blender or mini food processor and puree with the butter until very smooth. Taste and adjust with salt and pepper.

HOW TO MAKE THE MUSHROOM DUXELLE: Place a skillet over high heat, and when hot, add 1 tablespoon of olive oil. Add the garlic, mushrooms, and thyme. Sauté without stirring over high heat until one side begins to color and becomes slightly crusty. Season with salt and pepper. Reduce the heat to medium-high, flip the mushrooms to their uncooked side, and finish cooking. Set aside at room temperature to cool. Finely chop the mushrooms.

HOW TO MAKE THE HALIBUT CHEEK WELLINGTON: Cut the puff pastry sheet into 4½ x 4½-inch squares. Spread 1 tablespoon of mushroom duxelle onto the center of each puff pastry square. Place a small slice of foie gras on top of the mushroom duxelle. Place 1 whole halibut cheek on top of the foie gras. Place an additional tablespoon of duxelle on top of the cheek. Pull all four corners of the pastry over the halibut cheek and seal at the seams. Brush with egg wash (1 egg mixed with 1 tablespoon water). Repeat for 4 Wellingtons.

How to plate: Bake the halibut cheek Wellingtons at 350°F for 10 minutes, or until golden. Place 2 tablespoons of the fennel sauce in the middle of each plate. Dress the organic greens with the hazelnut vinaigrette and divide evenly between the four plates. Place each Wellington over the fennel sauce and serve immediately.

MAKES 4 SERVINGS

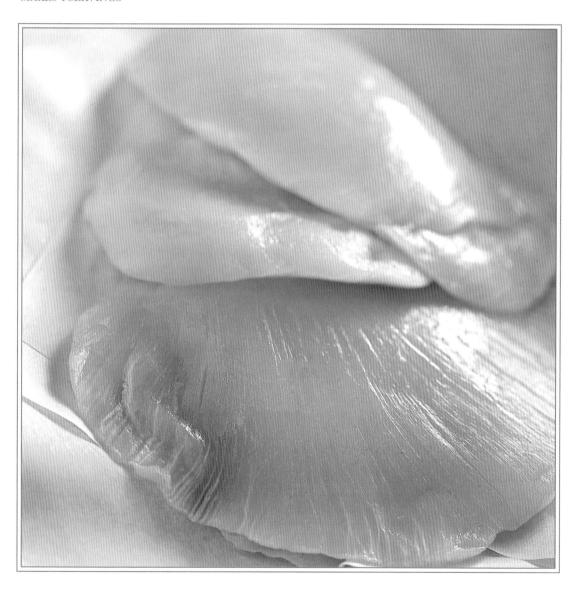

Halibut Cheek Stew with Heirloom Tomatoes, Cucumber, and Basil

1 cucumber
6 large heirloom tomatoes
  (variety of colors)
4 tablespoons extra-virgin
  olive oil
3 cloves garlic, finely sliced
4 halibut cheeks
Pinch salt and pepper
½ cup chopped fresh basil
8 kalamata olives (optional)
Salt and pepper, to taste

HOW TO MAKE THE HALIBUT STEW: Bring a small pot of salted water to a boil. Peel and remove the seeds from the cucumber. Using a paring knife, round the corners of the cucumber and slice, creating 1½-inch football-shaped pieces. Blanch the cucumbers in the boiling water for 30 seconds. Remove the cucumbers and immediately cool in an ice bath to stop the cooking process. Now remove the stems from the tomatoes and slice a shallow (x-shaped) cross-cut in the bottom of each tomato. Using the same blanching pot, blanch the tomatoes for 20 seconds and immediately cool in an ice bath.

Remove the skins from the tomatoes and chop into 2-inch pieces. Place a large skillet over high heat; when hot, add the olive oil. Add the garlic and heat for 1 minute. Add the tomatoes. Continue to cook until tomatoes soften, about 3 minutes. Add the halibut cheeks and cook at a low simmer for 10 minutes. Season with salt and pepper. Stir in the basil and cucumbers.

HOW TO PLATE: Divide the halibut cheek stew among four bowls. Garnish with a drizzle of olive oil, kalamata olives, or chopped basil.

MAKES 4 SERVINGS

Halibut Cheeks with Garden Mache, Wild Mushrooms, Fingerling Potatoes, and Bacon Vinaigrette

For the Bacon Vinaigrette

⅓ cup thinly sliced thick-cut bacon (about 3 slices)
¼ cup thinly sliced, peeled shallots
1 teaspoon minced fresh garlic
¼ cup sherry vinegar
⅓ cup extra-virgin olive oil

For the Wild Mushrooms and Fingerling Potatoes

8 ounces trumpet or porcini mushrooms, trimmed and sliced (¼ inch thick)
8 ounces chanterelle mushrooms, trimmed and sliced (¼ inch thick)
3 tablespoons olive oil, divided
Pinch kosher salt
4 fingerling potatoes, cooked and peeled
¼ cup French-style vinaigrette (bottled is okay)
4 ounces mache (or other small salad green), washed and dried

HOW TO MAKE THE BACON VINAIGRETTE: Combine the bacon and shallots in a large skillet and place over medium heat. Cook until the bacon renders its fat and the shallots soften and turn translucent, about 10 minutes. Add the garlic and cook another 2 minutes. Add the sherry vinegar and cook until the liquid is reduced to about 1 tablespoon. The mixture will smell strongly of bacon and pungent vinegar. Transfer the warm mixture to a blender or food processor and puree until smooth, stopping the machine to scrape down the sides several times. Add the olive oil and run the machine for 2 or 3 minutes to create a smooth vinaigrette. The dressing will be thick. Set aside at room temperature or refrigerate (for up to 2 weeks) if making in advance.

HOW TO MAKE THE WILD MUSHROOMS: Clean the mushrooms with damp paper towels or use a paring knife to lightly scrape off any loose dirt. Place a skillet over high heat; when hot, add 1 tablespoon of oil. Sauté the mushrooms without stirring over high heat until one side begins to color and becomes slightly crusty. Season with a pinch of kosher salt. Reduce the heat to medium-high, flip the mushrooms to their uncooked side, and finish cooking. Set aside at room temperature.

HOW TO MAKE THE FINGERLING POTATOES: Peel the fingerlings and cut into ¼-inch slices. Drizzle the potatoes with some of the French vinaigrette; set them aside while you proceed with the recipe.

HOW TO MAKE THE MACHE: Place the mache (or other small salad green) in a bowl and toss with 2 tablespoons of the bacon vinaigrette.

How to make the halibut cheeks: Place a large skillet over high heat; when hot, add 1 tablespoon of olive oil. Season the halibut cheeks with salt and pepper and place in the hot pan. Sauté until golden brown and flip, approximately 2 minutes per side.

How to assemble and plate: Place a large skillet over high heat and when hot, add 1 tablespoon of olive oil. Combine all of the mushrooms and sauté, stirring frequently, to reheat and crisp the mushrooms, about 2 minutes. Reduce the heat to medium. Add the shallots, garlic, pepper, parsley, and tarragon, and stir to combine. Cook for 1 minute, stirring constantly, then add 2 or 3 tablespoons of bacon vinaigrette to deglaze the pan. Remove from the heat and immediately pour the mushroom mixture over the mache. Add the potato slices and toss gently to combine the ingredients. Divide the salad among four plates, place a seared halibut cheek over the top of each plate, and serve immediately.

MAKES 4 SERVINGS

For the Halibut Cheeks
1 tablespoon olive oil
4 halibut cheeks
Pinch salt and pepper, to taste

For the Assembly
1 tablespoon olive oil
2 teaspoons minced shallots
1 teaspoon minced fresh garlic
$1/4$ teaspoon freshly ground pepper, or to taste
2 teaspoons minced fresh Italian parsley
2 teaspoons minced fresh tarragon

"Don't be put off by the instructions to cook mushrooms over high heat. Mushrooms are about 80 percent water, and the flesh needs to be broken down to release the juices and flavors inside. The easiest and quickest way to do that is with heat. When a mushroom encounters heat, the juices begin to rush out, which could cause the mushrooms to steam and become soggy. The way to avoid this is to start with a very hot pan and use a fat (in this case olive oil) that can withstand high temperatures without burning. If you add the mushrooms and allow them to sear and brown, undisturbed by stirring, they will caramelize beautifully and release their meaty flavor."

Miso Halibut Cheeks with Lime and Braised Bok Choy

For the Miso
1 ¼ cups granulated sugar
²/₃ cup mirin
²/₃ cup sake
1 cup white miso
3 tablespoons lime juice

For the Bok Choy
2 medium bok choy
2 tablespoons butter
½ cup chicken stock

For the Halibut Cheeks
1 cup potato starch
Pinch salt and pepper
4 halibut cheeks
2 cups peanut oil (or
    grapeseed oil)

HOW TO MAKE THE MISO: In a small pot, combine the sugar, mirin, and sake. Bring to a low simmer. Gradually add the white miso and stir to combine. Simmer for 10 minutes. Remove from the heat and stir in the lime juice.

HOW TO BRAISE THE BOK CHOY: Halve each bok choy and remove the lower portion (bottom) of each bulb. Next, bring a large saucepan to medium-high heat. Add the butter and place the bok choy inner side down. After 1 minute, turn the bok choy over. Add the chicken stock. Continue to heat until the bok choy is nicely glazed and soft, about 4 minutes.

HOW TO MAKE THE HALIBUT CHEEKS: Season the potato starch with salt and pepper. Dredge the halibut cheeks in the starch. In a large pot, heat the peanut oil to about 400°F. Gently place the halibut cheeks in the oil and fry until golden, about 3 minutes.

HOW TO PLATE: Place 2 tablespoons of miso sauce in the center of four small plates. Place one half of a bok choy in the middle of each plate. Drizzle with the remaining pan juices. Place one halibut cheek over each plate of bok choy.

MAKES 4 SERVINGS

"Having the correct knife for the job is half the game in cooking. Cutting herbs into a fine chiffonade, for instance, is best accomplished with a very sharp, thin-bladed knife. The thinner the actual edge of the blade, the easier it is to make very fine slices. With herbs, it's important to slice [julienne] rather than roughly chop. Chopping bruises the herbs and causes the juices to release. As a result, much of the flavor of the herbs will be left behind on your chopping board."

Olive Oil Poached Halibut Cheeks with Red Beet Soup, Arugula Gnocchi, and Horseradish Cream

For the Horseradish Cream
3 tablespoons crème fraiche
1 tablespoon prepared
  horseradish (or 1
  tablespoon finely grated
  fresh horseradish)
1 teaspoon fresh lime juice
Pinch salt and freshly ground
  pepper, to taste

For the Red Beet Soup
1¼ pounds baby red beets,
  washed and trimmed
2 tablespoons canola oil
2 tablespoons sherry vinegar
½ bunch fresh thyme (or 1
  tablespoon dried thyme)
1 small yellow onion,
  quartered
Salt and pepper, to taste
1 tablespoon olive oil
1½ cups thinly sliced yellow
  (sweet) onion
2 cloves garlic, thinly sliced
½ cup white wine
2-4 cups vegetable stock

For the Arugula Gnocchi
(makes 36)
8 ounces baby arugula
½ cup water
¾ cup ricotta cheese
½ cup finely grated
  Parmesan cheese
½ cup finely grated Pecorino
  Romano cheese
1 large egg, beaten and
  divided
¼ teaspoon white pepper
Freshly grated nutmeg, to
  taste
½ cup all-purpose flour

HOW TO MAKE THE HORSERADISH CREAM: Combine the crème fraiche, horseradish, and lime juice in a small bowl and whisk to blend. Season to taste with salt and pepper. Refrigerate until serving time.

HOW TO MAKE THE RED BEET SOUP: Position a rack in the middle of the oven and preheat to 350°F. Place beets in a baking pan and toss with the canola oil, sherry vinegar, thyme, and quartered onion. Season with salt and pepper. Cover the pan tightly with aluminum foil and roast the beets until they are very tender, 45 to 60 minutes. Cool completely, then peel.

Heat a large deep skillet over medium heat and add the olive oil. Add the sliced onions and cook for 10 minutes, stirring occasionally. Add the garlic and cook another 5 minutes. The vegetables should only color slightly, so adjust heat accordingly. Pour in the wine and raise the heat to medium-high. Cook until the wine is almost evaporated, 3 to 5 minutes. Add the beets and 2 cups of stock. Simmer for 5 minutes, then transfer the contents of the pan to a food processor or blender and puree until very smooth. The soup will possibly be too thick, so thin with vegetable stock to the consistency of heavy cream.

HOW TO MAKE THE GNOCCHI: Place the arugula in a large skillet with ½ cup of water and cook over high heat until the arugula wilts, 3 to 5 minutes. It may be necessary to do this in 2 batches. Drain, and when cool, thoroughly squeeze dry. Finely chop the arugula and place in a medium bowl. Next, add the ricotta, grated cheeses, half of the beaten egg, the pepper, and nutmeg to the bowl. Stir to blend. The mixture can then be covered and refrigerated for 1 day.

When ready to form the gnocchi, bring a large pot of salted water to a slow simmer. Transfer the beet soup to another saucepan and bring to a simmer over medium heat. Keep the soup warm while you cook the gnocchi.

Lightly flour a counter or board. Flour your hands and gently roll about 1 tablespoon of the ricotta mixture between your palms, forming 1½-inch-long dumplings. Roll the gnocchis in the flour to lightly coat them. Carefully transfer 10 or 12 gnocchis to the simmering water and cook until they float. Remove them with a slotted spoon as soon as they rise to the surface, placing them on a large plate to cool and firm. Do not let the water boil or the gnocchis will break apart. Repeat in small batches with the remaining dough.

HOW TO MAKE THE POACHED HALIBUT: In a large pot, heat the butter to 160°F. Gently add the halibut cheeks and slowly poach for 10 minutes. Remove and gently slice.

HOW TO PLATE: Place a dollop of horseradish cream in the center of each bowl. Arrange 1 sliced halibut cheek and 5 or 6 warm gnocchi atop the cream. Drizzle with a bit of olive oil, then place a chervil or parsley leaf on top of the raft of gnocchi.

Remove the soup from the heat and stir in 1 tablespoon of extra-virgin olive oil. Pour the soup into a pitcher or container with a spout. Arrange the soup plates on the table at each place setting, then carefully pour a ring of red beet soup around the gnocchi.

MAKES 4 SERVINGS

For the Poached Halibut
½ pound butter
4 halibut cheeks

For the Garnish
Extra-virgin olive oil
4 fresh chervil or Italian
   parsley leaves

"Peeling beets is a chore, and a messy one at that. Use rubber or disposable gloves if you don't want to stain your hands. I use a terry cloth kitchen towel to remove beet skins because a paring knife nicks the beet and spoils its shape. While appearances are not important for this soup because the beets are pureed, in a salad you might want the beets to be unblemished. Rub the beets with the towel and the skins will slip off. It is best to do this over a sink or large bowl to keep cleanup to a minimum. Devote your towel to kitchen chores such as peeling beets and wringing moisture from blanched or cooked greens."

"Here in Kodiak, Alaska, we have a great fishery management program in place to ensure all of our seafood is sustainable. As a chef who strongly supports seafood sustainability, cooking with the 'right' fish is very important to me."

—Executive Chef Joel Chenet

Chapter 11

SOLE (PACIFIC DOVER)

EXECUTIVE CHEF JOEL CHENET, "AMBASSADOR OF SUSTAINABLE SEAFOOD"—MILL BAY COFFEE AND PASTRY

*T*he cold, crisp waters of Alaska are home to some of the most prized species of sole, a small flatfish that inhabits many areas of Alaska. One of these species is the Pacific Dover sole.

Not to be confused with the European Dover sole, the Pacific Dover sole is a deep-water flatfish with a long, slender body that reaches 12 to 30 inches in length. Actually a member of the flounder family, the Pacific Dover sole is commercially harvested in Alaska by trawlers and landed primarily at night when the sole comes out of the sand where it buries itself during the day.

Pacific Dover sole is typically sold as fillets with the skin off. Like most Alaskan soles, Pacific Dover sole is mild with a sweet flavor. The sole's texture is firm, lean yet delicate. The meat, which is available year-round, should be glistening white and will remain white when cooked.

Chef Joel Chenet's culinary résumé reads like a well-worn passport. In his native France, Chef Chenet cut his teeth in the kitchens of numerous three- and four-star hotels and was honored as the country's "Best Young Chef." He went on to work in numerous places in Europe and Africa before heading to the United States. In the United States he was the chef for the French president and the French Consulate before becoming sous-chef of The Pierre. He opened the kitchen at the first U.S. Relais and Châteaux hotel, cooked at properties operated by Dunfey Hotels (now Omni Hotels), and worked as executive chef of the Buffalo Club in Buffalo, New York.

Recently, Chef Chenet, who now lives in Alaska, attained the title "Ambassador of Sustainable Seafood" and holds the 2008 Sustainable Seafood Challenge "Most Original" award for his creative contest entries during the Monterey Bay Aquarium's Cooking for Solutions event series.

Pacific Sole with Hot-Smoked Salmon and Lox

2 ounces hot-smoked
    Alaskan salmon
4 ounces soft cream cheese
1 teaspoon dry dill
1/4 teaspoon Cajun spices
8 fresh Pacific sole fillets
4 slices wild Alaskan salmon
    lox, cut in two
Salt and pepper to taste
1 tablespoon olive oil
1 tablespoon butter
2 tablespoons finely
    chopped shallots
1/2 cup vodka
1 cup heavy whipping cream
8 teaspoons salmon caviar
    (optional)
4 sprigs fresh dill, for garnish

HOW TO MAKE THE SOLE: Finely chop the smoked salmon and mix with the cream cheese, dry dill, and Cajun spices. Combine well.

Pat dry the sole fillets with paper towels. Arrange the fillets side by side on a cutting board. Spread the smoked salmon cream cheese spread equally on each fillet. Then place a slice of lox on top of each fillet. Fold each fillet, and secure with toothpicks. Season with salt and pepper.

In a sauté pan, add the oil and butter, and heat over medium-high heat. When hot, add the sole fillets and cook about 2 minutes on each side. Add the shallots to the pan and cook for 1 minute. Flambé the pan with vodka (note: use extreme caution when igniting alcohol). Remove the fillets from the pan and reserve.

Add the heavy cream to the pan and reduce by half. Check the seasoning.

HOW TO PLATE: On four warm serving plates, arrange 2 sole fillets per plate. Top with the sauce, and garnish with the salmon caviar and fresh dill.

MAKES 4 SERVINGS

"I enjoy Alaskan sole because it's very mild in flavor, easy to prepare . . . and children love eating it!"

Pacific Sole with Clam Bacon Butter and Lemon

1 dozen live littleneck
"steamer" clams
1 stick butter, softened
2 medium shallots, finely
chopped
½ red bell pepper, diced
small
1 lemon, juiced and divided
2 tablespoons chopped fresh
chives
Salt, to taste
Pinch cayenne pepper
3 slices smoked bacon,
julienned
1 cup white bread crumbs
2 tablespoons chopped fresh
parsley
8–10 fresh Pacific sole fillets,
depending on size
Salt and pepper, to taste
½ cup dry white wine
1 lemon, for garnish

HOW TO MAKE THE SOLE: Begin by opening the raw clams, removing the clam meat, and chopping the clams. Reserve the juice.

In a bowl, add the chopped clam meat, along with the clam juice, soft butter, shallots, red bell pepper, juice of half a lemon, chives, salt, cayenne pepper, and bacon.

Mix the bread crumbs with the chopped parsley. Pat dry the sole fillets, and season with salt and pepper.

In a greased baking dish, add the white wine. Arrange the sole fillets on top of the wine and spread the clam and butter spread on each fillet. Top with a generous sprinkling of bread crumbs. Squeeze the juice from the other half of the lemon over the sole. Bake at 375°F for 10 to 12 minutes.

HOW TO PLATE: Transfer the sole to a warm dinner platter and top the fillets with the baking juices. Garnish with lemon slices or wedges.

MAKES 4 SERVINGS

"The number one rule to remember in seafood cookery is not to overcook the fish. Sole is particularly delicate and tender, so cook carefully. It won't take long."

DEEPWATER FISH

Pacific Sole with Vegetable Juice and Peanut Butter

HOW TO MAKE THE SOLE: In a bowl, combine the flour, cumin, coriander, and salt and pepper. Dredge each sole fillet in the seasoned flour.

In a hot, nonstick sauté pan, add the oil and sauté the sole fillets 2 to 3 minutes on each side, or until golden brown. Remove the sole fillets from the pan and reserve in a warm place, such as the oven.

To the sauté pan, add the garlic and chopped onion, browning slightly. Add the lemon juice and V8 juice. Cook for 2 minutes. Add the peanut butter, stirring well with a wooden spoon. Season with salt and pepper, to taste.

HOW TO PLATE: Divide the sole fillets on four dinner plates. Top with the sauce and sprinkle with chopped scallions. Serve with rice or sweet potatoes.

MAKES 4 SERVINGS

1/2 cup all-purpose flour
1/2 teaspoon ground cumin
1/2 teaspoon ground coriander
Salt and pepper, to taste
8–10 fresh Pacific sole fillets
1/4 cup olive oil
1 tablespoon chopped garlic
1 cup finely chopped onion
1 lemon, juiced
1 cup spicy V8 juice
1/4 cup peanut butter
2 scallions, finely cut (green part only)

Pacific Sole with Garden Vegetables and Pesto Spaghetti

For the Pesto
2 cups fresh basil leaves
5 fresh garlic cloves
1/2 cup olive oil
2 tablespoons toasted pine
 nuts
1 tablespoon fresh lemon
 juice
Pinch salt and pepper, to
 taste

For the Sole
4 ounces uncooked
 spaghetti
1/2 cup olive oil, divided
1/4 cup pesto, see recipe
 above
1 large vine tomato, peeled,
 seeded, and chopped
2 medium zucchini
2 medium carrots
2 tablespoons white
 balsamic vinegar
1 tablespoon chopped garlic
Salt and pepper, to taste
Red pepper flakes, to taste
8–10 fresh Pacific sole fillets
8–10 fresh basil leaves
5 slices prosciutto, cut in two
 lengthwise
1/2 cup vermouth
6 ounces butter

HOW TO MAKE THE PESTO: Simply combine the basil, garlic, olive oil, pine nuts, lemon juice, and salt and pepper in a food processor. Blend until smooth. Reserve.

HOW TO MAKE THE SOLE: Cook the spaghetti al dente according to package directions. Drain and coat with half the olive oil. Toss with the fresh pesto and chopped tomatoes and reserve.

Using a mandoline, make long zucchini and carrot julienne. Transfer to a bowl and combine with the vinegar and garlic. Season to taste with salt and pepper and sprinkle a few red pepper flakes. Add the spaghetti and gently toss. Keep warm.

Pat dry the sole fillets, and arrange side by side on a cutting board. Season with salt and pepper. Place a basil leaf and a piece of prosciutto on each fillet. Fold the fillets and secure with toothpicks.

In a nonstick sauté pan, add the remaining olive oil. When hot, arrange the sole fillets and cook 2 minutes on each side. Remove the fillets and deglaze the pan with vermouth. Reduce and add the butter, stirring well with a wooden spoon.

HOW TO PLATE: Make a nest of spaghetti on each plate, arrange sole fillet on top, and top with the sauce.

MAKES 4 SERVINGS

"Sometimes I have to remind myself fish quantities are different here in Kodiak. I remember last year visiting a fishery to obtain some sole for a large dinner party for 100 people. The manager called the dock foreman to accompany me to the boat. Onboard were over 20,000 pounds of freshly caught sole! The foreman asked me how many fish I would need. I had to laugh. Let's just say I found what I needed."

Pacific Sole with Leek and Swiss Cheese

HOW TO MAKE THE SOLE: Julienne the leeks and wash well. Place in a saucepan with ½ cup of white wine, 2 tablespoons butter, and the clam juice. Cook until the leeks are tender. Strain and reserve the liquid.

In a saucepan, make a roux with the remaining butter and flour. Cook for 3 minutes. Add the remaining white wine along with the garlic, shallots, leek juice, bay leaf, thyme, and cream. Stir well and cook 10 to 15 minutes over medium heat. Season with salt and pepper, and strain through a sieve.

Pat dry the sole fillets and season with salt and pepper.

In a greased baking pan, add half the sauce, sprinkle half of the leek julienne and half the Swiss cheese, and arrange the seasoned sole fillets on top. Top the fillets with the remaining sauce, leeks, and Swiss cheese. Bake in a 375°F oven for 15 minutes.

HOW TO PLATE: Divide the layered sole among four warm individual serving plates and serve immediately.

MAKES 4 SERVINGS

2 leeks, white part only
1½ cups white wine, divided
5 tablespoons butter, divided
1 cup clam juice
4 tablespoons all-purpose flour
1 tablespoon chopped garlic
2 tablespoons chopped shallots
1 bay leaf
1 sprig fresh thyme
2 cups light cream
Salt and pepper, to taste
8–10 fresh Pacific sole fillets
1½ cups grated Swiss cheese

"Alaska offers the best when it comes to well-managed seafood. I've been following such sustainable practices since I started cooking more than 30 years ago."

—Executive Chef Bradley Ogden

Chapter 12

SOLE (YELLOWFIN)

EXECUTIVE CHEF BRADLEY OGDEN—THE LARK CREEK RESTAURANT GROUP

*Y*ellowfin (or yellow) sole is one of the smallest of soles and one of the most abundant flatfish in the eastern Bering Sea. Yellowfin sole makes up one of the largest flatfish fisheries in the United States. Yellowfin sole are highly valued for their delicate, mild flavor and tender texture. As with many Alaska fish, the yellowfin sole is lean, low in fat, and high in protein. Best of all, yellowfin sole is available year-round.

Yellowfin sole are a relatively slow-growing and long-lived species. They tend to concentrate on the outer continental shelf during winter and move to shallow water to feed and spawn in the summer. They are harvested by trawl gear and are managed as a shallow-water species, unlike Alaska's other species of sole.

Chef Bradley Ogden's philosophy of "keeping it simple" and using the freshest ingredients available has helped him become one of the most respected names in the culinary industry.

Chef Ogden is the creator of several award-winning restaurants, including Lark Creek Inn in Marin County, One Market in San Francisco, Bradley Ogden at Caesar's Palace in Las Vegas, and Root 246 in Solvang, California. In 2004, Bradley Ogden at Caesar's Palace received the "Best New Restaurant" award from the James Beard Foundation.

> "I enjoy cooking with sole plucked from the icy waters of Alaska. The fish is very low in fat and the texture and quality of Alaskan sole is unrivaled. It truly is the poor man's lobster."

Other prestigious honors that Chef Ogden has received over the last thirty years include "Best Chef of California" by the James Beard Foundation, one of the "Great American Chefs" by the International Wine and Food Society, the "Golden Plate Award" by the American Academy of Achievement, and "Chef of the Year" by the Culinary Institute of America.

Crispy Sole with Roasted Spaghetti Squash "Noodles" and Charred Cava Cava Orange Sauce

For the Roasted Spaghetti Squash "Noodles"

3 cardamom pods, white
1/2 teaspoon allspice, whole
3 star anise, whole
1 1/2–2 pounds spaghetti
    squash
3 tablespoons unsalted
    butter
2 tablespoons honey
2 tablespoons brown sugar
1 teaspoon kosher salt
1 teaspoon fresh ground
    black pepper
2 tart apples
1 lemon, juiced
1/2 cup apple cider (optional)

For the Cava Cava Orange Sauce (makes 3 cups)

2 cava cava oranges, peeled
1/4 cup olive oil
1 tablespoon kosher salt,
    divided
1 teaspoon fresh ground
    black pepper, divided
1/4 cup grapeseed oil
1/4 cup citrus juice from
    lemon and orange
1/4 cup minced red onion
1 teaspoon dijon mustard
2 tablespoons minced chives
2 tablespoons chopped
    Italian parsley
1 tablespoon chopped chervil

HOW TO MAKE THE ROASTED SPAGHETTI SQUASH "NOODLES": Preheat the oven to 300°F.

Put the cardamom pods, allspice, and star anise in a sauté pan. Place over low-medium heat and toast lightly. Remove and grind in a spice grinder. Next, cut the spaghetti squash lengthwise. Scoop out the seeds, pulp, and discard. Place the squash on a baking sheet pan or a casserole dish, skin side down. Melt the butter and brush onto the flesh of the squash. Sprinkle the spices over the squash, drizzle the honey and brown sugar, and season with the salt and pepper. Slice the apples in half and place in a bowl. Add the lemon juice and toss. Place one half of the apple into the cavity of each piece of squash. Add the apple cider. Place in the middle rack of the oven and bake for 1½ to 2 hours or until fork tender (basting occasionally). Remove the squash from the oven, discard the apples and let cool. Using a fork, scrape the cooked squash to make noodles, and reserve for the finished dish.

Note: To re-warm the squash, place in a skillet with butter, salt, and pepper and place in a preheated 400°F oven for 8 to 10 minutes.

HOW TO MAKE THE CAVA CAVA SAUCE: Preheat an outdoor grill to high. Place the two oranges on a large sheet of aluminum foil, drizzle with the olive oil, and season with ¼ teaspoon salt and ¼ teaspoon pepper; wrap. Place over the hot grill and grill until soft and charred lightly, turning often (should take about 15 minutes). Remove and let cool slightly. Puree oranges in a food processor until smooth. Place in bowl. Combine with the grapeseed oil, citrus juice, red onion, dijon mustard, chives, parsley, and chervil. Adjust with salt and pepper and reserve for saucing the sole.

How to make the crispy sole: Pat dry the sole fillets with paper towels and season with salt and pepper. Place two large stainless steel or cast-iron skillets over a hot burner and add the grapeseed oil evenly to both. Heat until almost smoking. Place the fillets skin side down and sauté 2 minutes, or until crispy and lightly brown. Turn the heat down to low, and use a fish spatula to turn the fillets over. Add the rosemary, butter, zest, and lemon juice. Baste the fillets, cooking another couple of minutes. Remove the fillets and drain on paper towels.

How to plate: Remove the warm spaghetti squash with a fork and twirl like you would pasta. Place a portion in the centers of four rectangle plates. Place one fillet over the "noodles" lengthwise to cover. Spoon out and drizzle the cava cava sauce (¼ cup per dish) and serve.

MAKES 4 SERVINGS

For the Crispy Sole

4 8-ounce fillets fresh sole, skin on and scored, boneless
1½ teaspoons kosher salt
1 teaspoon fresh ground black pepper
½ cup grapeseed oil
2 fresh rosemary sprigs
3 tablespoons butter, unsalted
1 orange, zested
2 lemons, juiced

Sole with Leek and Sweet Potato "Risotto"

For the Leek and Sweet Potato "Risotto"
2 pounds sweet potatoes,
 peeled and cut into ½-inch
 dice, soaked in cold water
2 tablespoons olive oil
2 tablespoons unsalted
 butter
4 cups ¼-inch diced leeks,
 use mostly the white part
 and a little green
5 cups vegetable stock
Kosher salt
Fresh ground black pepper
Lemon juice

For the Sole
½ cup grapeseed oil
1½ pounds sole fillets,
 scaled and boned, cut into
 3-ounce bias cuts, 2 per
 serving
Kosher salt
Fresh ground black pepper
4 tablespoons unsalted
 butter
3 2-inch pieces thyme sprigs
2 lemons, zested, segmented,
 and juiced
3 tangerines, zested and
 segmented
1 cup pea shoots, toasted in
 olive oil and lemon juice
2 tablespoons extra-virgin
 olive oil

HOW TO MAKE THE LEEK AND SWEET POTATO "RISOTTO": Drain the sweet potatoes. In a heavy-bottomed 1 gallon stainless steel saucepan, add the olive oil and butter, and melt over low heat. Add the sweet potatoes and leeks. Cover and let sweat for 15 minutes, stirring occasionally. Remove the cover, and add the vegetable stock very slowly, as when cooking a risotto, stirring continuously over a 15-minute period (on low heat) until the stock has been absorbed and cooked out. Season with salt and pepper. Add 1 teaspoon of lemon juice and reserve the rest for the finished dish.

HOW TO MAKE THE SOLE: In two large stainless steel or cast-iron sauté pans, add enough grapeseed oil to come up to ⅛-inch level and heat over a high fire until very hot. Season the sole fillets with salt and pepper. Place skin side down in the hot oil, and sauté until crispy, about 2 to 3 minutes. Using a fish spatula, remove the fillets and drain on paper towels. Discard the oil from the pan. Lower the heat, and add the butter and thyme sprigs. Brown the butter lightly and froth up. Add the citrus juice and zest from the lemons and tangerines, and spoon over the fillets.

HOW TO PLATE: Portion the "risotto" into individual soup plates. Arrange the sole fillets on top. In a bowl, combine the lemon and tangerine segments and pea shoots, season with salt and pepper, and drizzle a little extra-virgin olive oil and lemon juice to coat. Sprinkle over the fillets and "risotto" and serve.

MAKES 4 SERVINGS

Sole Jambalaya

For the Jambalaya

2 tablespoons olive oil

4 ounces andouille sausage, quartered lengthwise and cut into ³/₄-inch pieces (about 1 cup)

2 medium stalks celery, cut into ¹/₄-inch slices (about 1 cup)

1 medium carrot, peeled and cut into ¹/₂-inch pieces (about ¹/₂ cup)

2 medium yellow Spanish onions, cut into ¹/₂-inch dice (about 2 cups)

³/₄ cup Carolina short grain rice, rinsed under cold water and drained

1¹/₂ tablespoons peeled and minced garlic

2 cups peeled, seeded, and chopped tomatoes

1 teaspoon minced fresh thyme

2 tablespoons balsamic vinegar

1 teaspoon gumbo file

1 teaspoon fresh black pepper

5 cups tomato ham hock broth

Zest from 2 lemons, and juiced

¹/₄ cup chopped Italian parsley

2 teaspoons kosher salt

HOW TO MAKE THE JAMBALAYA: Preheat the oven to 350°F. Heat the olive oil in a heavy-bottomed, ovenproof 4-quart stockpot or brassier. Add the andouille sausage and sauté for a few minutes until sausage is lightly browned. Turn heat down slightly. Add the celery, carrots, onions, rice, and garlic and sauté for another minute or two. Add the chopped tomatoes, thyme, balsamic vinegar, gumbo file, black pepper, 5 cups of the tomato ham hock broth, and lemon zest. Cover pan, place in the middle of the oven, and cook for 20 to 25 minutes or until rice is cooked. Remove from oven and add the parsley and salt. Adjust seasoning, if needed.

"Alaskan sole is extremely versatile, and can be used in a number of ways, from fish stews to elegant preparations. Sole also does well with simple braises and reduction sauces. . . .

"When purchasing fresh seafood, it is wise to keep a cooler in the car so your seafood will not spoil, especially during long commutes home. When preparing your fish, keep the seafood on ice and always use the fish in a timely fashion, if not right away."

How to make the sole: In a large 12-inch stainless steel sauté pan, add the olive oil and grapeseed oil, and heat the oil over a very hot flame. Sauté the sole fillets until crispy on the flesh side, about 2 or 3 minutes. Turn the fillets over and drain fat. Add the butter. Baste fish and remove from pan. Place onto a paper towel to drain.

How to plate: Spoon the jambalaya mixture into the center of four large serving bowls. Top with the sole fillets, sprinkle with tasso, and serve.

MAKES 4 SERVINGS

For the Sole
3 tablespoons olive oil
3 tablespoons grapeseed oil
4 5-ounce boneless fillets sole, rubbed with olive oil, salt, and pepper
3 tablespoons unsalted butter
1 ounce tasso, julienned and lightly sautéed in olive oil and drained (about 2 tablespoons)

Herb-Crusted Sole with Lentil Salad and Pancetta Vinaigrette

For the Herb Crust (makes 2 cups)
5 tablespoons unsalted butter
3 garlic cloves, crushed
1 tablespoon dijon mustard
2 cups fresh white bread crumbs
1/4 cup finely chopped Italian parsley
1/4 cup minced chives
2 tablespoons finely chopped tarragon
1 teaspoon kosher salt
1/2 teaspoon fresh ground black pepper

For the Sole
1/2 teaspoon dried thyme
3 cloves fresh garlic, peeled and cut into slivers
1/2 teaspoon lemon zest
Kosher salt
Fresh ground black pepper
Dijon mustard
4 6-ounce sole fillets, boneless and skinless
1/4 cup olive oil

For the Lentil Salad
1 1/2 cups lentils
1/4 cup olive oil
1/2 cup minced celery
4 cups water
1 teaspoon kosher salt
3 tablespoons red wine vinegar
1/3 cup extra-virgin olive oil
1/4 teaspoon fresh ground black pepper

HOW TO MAKE THE HERB CRUST FOR THE SOLE: In a 1-quart stainless steel saucepan, add the butter and garlic. Melt the butter over low heat, cover, and cook for 5 minutes. Turn off the heat and let stand for 10 minutes. Strain and discard the garlic from the butter.

In a large bowl, add the dijon mustard and whisk in the garlic butter. Add the bread crumbs, Italian parsley, chives, tarragon, salt, and pepper. Mix well. Reserve for the fish.

HOW TO MAKE THE SOLE: Using the back of a knife, crush together the thyme, garlic, lemon zest, 1 teaspoon kosher salt, and 1/2 teaspoon black pepper. Rub the sole pieces with the herb mixture and 1/4 cup olive oil. Cover and marinate for several hours or overnight in the refrigerator.

Preheat the broiler. Brush a sheet pan with olive oil and add the sole fillets. Season the sole with salt and pepper, and brush lightly with dijon mustard on top. Sprinkle with the herb crust and pat evenly to create a thin crust. Place under broiler, until golden brown and crispy. Turn the pan occasionally to cook evenly, approximately 6 to 8 minutes.

HOW TO MAKE THE LENTIL SALAD: Wash the lentils in cold water and drain. In a 6-quart saucepan, heat the 1/4 cup olive oil over medium heat. Add the minced celery and sauté, stirring occasionally for 5 minutes. Add the lentils, water, and salt. Bring to a simmer. Lower the heat, cover, and simmer until the lentils are just tender (anywhere from 45 minutes to 1 1/2 hours depending on the lentils). Add more water during the cooking if necessary. Drain the cooked lentils and season with the vinegar, olive oil, salt, and pepper. Keep warm until ready to serve.

HOW TO MAKE THE PANCETTA VINAIGRETTE: Place the minced pancetta in a small pan over low heat and cook until the fat has rendered and the pancetta is light brown in color. Drain the pancetta on paper towels. In a small bowl, whisk together the rendered pancetta and the shallots, garlic, vinegar, olive oil, salt, and pepper.

HOW TO PLATE: Toss the arugula with the 1 tablespoon red wine vinegar and 3 tablespoons olive oil. Arrange on warm serving plates. Top with the warm lentil salad, the broiled sole, and several slices of grilled pancetta. Finish by spooning over the vinaigrette.

MAKES 4 SERVINGS

For the Pancetta Vinaigrette
3 thin slices pancetta, minced
2 shallots, minced
1 clove garlic, minced
3 tablespoons red wine vinegar
$1/3$ cup olive oil
$1/4$ teaspoon kosher salt
$1/4$ teaspoon fresh ground pepper
2 cups arugula, washed and dried
1 tablespoon red wine vinegar
3 tablespoons olive oil
12 slices pancetta, grilled

"As a native Alaskan, I feel it is vitally important to maintain Alaska's pristine waters and natural resources for generations to come. I have a great sense of pride when it comes to our beautiful state, and I am committed to do whatever I am able to in order to preserve our very special environment. I only use wild-caught Alaskan fish in our restaurant at the university and instill in our students the importance of promoting sustainability. I believe in supporting our local community as much as possible, and in turn I find myself supported in my business ventures as well."

—Executive Chef Naomi Everett

Chapter 13

YELLOW-EYE ROCKFISH

EXECUTIVE CHEF NAOMI EVERETT—UNIVERSITY OF ALASKA

*Y*ellow-eye rockfish range from northern Baja California to the Aleutian Islands, Alaska, but are most common from central California to the Gulf of Alaska. They are very large fish that reach up to 3.5 feet in length and 39 pounds in weight. Adults generally move into deeper water as they increase in size and age, selecting rocky bottoms and outcrops, and are most commonly found between 300 to 590 feet.

Yellow-eye rockfish are also among the longest lived of rockfishes, living up to 118 years. Rockfish are slow growing and do not reproduce until they are quite mature—some may be as old as 15 to 20 years before they reproduce! Maximum ages attained for some species can be as high as 150 years. Because of their slow growth, rockfish cannot be harvested at the rates fast-growing stocks such as salmon can withstand.

After traveling the United States and working in restaurants around the country, in 2005 Chef Naomi Everett took on the challenge of bringing fine dining to Alaska's Matanuska Valley and headed up the team at Settlers Bay Lodge in Wasilla, Alaska. In 2006 she won the Great Alaska Seafood Cook-off and that same year represented Alaska in the Great American Seafood Cook-off in New Orleans, where she was one of five chefs featured by the Food Network's coverage of the event.

Chef Everett has always believed in utilizing Alaska's amazing resources, from local produce to seafood, and has been working with the Alaska Seafood Marketing Institute (ASMI) to promote sustainable Alaskan seafood over the last few years, traveling to New York, New Orleans, and China, as well as

> "Alaska yellow-eye rockfish is a wonderful fish to work with. I love the way it retains moisture, and it has a firm texture and mild flavor."

belonging to the Wild Alaska Seafood Congress of Conscious Chefs. In the fall of 2007 Chef Everett accepted a full-time position with the University of Alaska as chef instructor of culinary arts.

Poached Alaska Yellow-Eye Rockfish with Butternut Squash/ Eggplant Hash and Carrot Cardamom Cream Sauce

For the Rockfish

8 3-ounce portions fresh Alaska yellow-eye rockfish

Pinch kosher salt and fresh ground pepper, to taste

2 tablespoons unsalted butter

1 large shallot, peeled, ends trimmed, and finely sliced

8 sliced lemon rounds, 1/8 inch thick

2 cups sauvignon blanc

4 sprigs fresh Italian parsley

For the Carrot Cardamom Cream Sauce (makes 2 cups)

1 cup sauvignon blanc

2 tablespoons roughly chopped shallot

1 teaspoon whole, toasted cardamom pods

1 teaspoon whole, toasted coriander seeds

1 pound carrots, peeled and large rough cut

1 quart heavy cream

1 small whole cinnamon stick

Pinch kosher salt and fresh ground white pepper, to taste

HOW TO MAKE THE ROCKFISH: Season each side of the rockfish with salt and pepper. Heat the butter in a large nonstick skillet, something that has a lid, over medium-high heat. Place the rockfish, presentation side down, into the skillet and quickly sear until color develops on the rockfish. Turn the pieces of fish over and immediately add the shallots, lemon rounds, parsley, and wine.

Bring to a quick boil, reduce to a gentle simmer, and cover. Simmer for 2 to 3 minutes, depending on how thick the fish is. Remove from heat and reserve.

HOW TO MAKE THE CARROT CARDAMOM CREAM SAUCE: Combine the wine and shallots in a medium saucepot and reduce by half over medium heat. Place the cardamom and coriander seeds inside a piece of cheesecloth or coffee filter, and place inside the pot to infuse the sauce.

Add the carrots, cream, and cinnamon stick to the pot, and simmer gently (be careful to not boil) until carrots are fork tender and cream has thickened (able to coat the back of a spoon). Once the carrots are cooked, remove the cardamom, coriander, and cinnamon stick, and discard. Using a blender, puree the carrots in the cream until smooth. Strain through a fine-mesh sieve and season with salt and pepper.

How to make the butternut squash and eggplant hash:
Preheat the oven to 375°F. Toss the squash with half of the olive oil, 2 sprigs of the thyme, and salt and pepper. Place on a baking sheet and roast until tender and slightly caramelized, about 15 to 20 minutes. Cook longer if needed. Remove from the oven and cool at room temperature, discarding the thyme sprigs. Repeat the same process as above with the eggplant. When the squash and eggplant have cooled, heat the clarified butter in a large sauté pan over medium-high heat. Add the mushrooms to the hot pan and sauté until they begin to caramelize and still look moist. Add the shallot, garlic, and a little salt and pepper; deglaze and flambé with the Madeira. Lower the heat to medium and add the roasted butternut squash and eggplant to the mushrooms, tossing well until warmed through and tender, and just beginning to hold together. The mixture should be nice and moist, not dry.

Remove from heat and season with salt and pepper. Serve immediately.

How to plate: Place the poached pieces of fish on top of the vegetable hash and ladle a small amount of the carrot cream sauce around the hash. Garnish with one of the poached lemon slices per plate and fresh Italian parsley sprigs, if desired. Repeat for all eight plates.

MAKES 8 SERVINGS

For the Butternut Squash and Eggplant Hash (makes 2¹/₂ cups)
2 cups peeled and medium-diced butternut squash
4 tablespoons extra-virgin olive oil
4 sprigs fresh thyme
Pinch kosher salt and fresh ground pepper, to taste
2 cups unpeeled and medium-diced eggplant
2 tablespoons clarified butter
1 cup shiitake mushrooms, stems removed and sliced ¹/₂ inch thick
1 tablespoon finely minced shallot
1 teaspoon finely minced garlic
¹/₂ ounce Madeira wine

"Clarified butter is a fantastic fat for this fish. The butter complements the yellow-eye's natural flavor without masking the fish."

Pan-Seared Alaska Yellow-Eye Rockfish with Warm Wild Mushroom Salad, Parsnip Puree, and Pumpkin Sauce

For the Rockfish

4 5-ounce portions fresh Alaska yellow-eye rockfish
Pinch kosher salt and fresh ground pepper, to taste
1½ pounds fresh shiitake, oyster, and morel mushrooms, cleaned, stems removed, and trimmed
2–4 tablespoons unsalted butter
1 tablespoon minced shallot
½ tablespoon minced garlic
1 teaspoon finely chopped fresh thyme
2 ounces brandy
2 tablespoons clarified butter (or vegetable oil)

For the Pumpkin Sauce

2 cups Gewürztraminer wine
2 tablespoons finely minced shallot
2 cups pumpkin puree
1 cup heavy whipping cream
Pinch kosher salt and fresh ground pepper, to taste

For the Parsnip Puree

1½ pounds fresh parsnips
¼ pound unsalted butter
1½ cups heavy cream
2 sprigs fresh rosemary
Pinch kosher salt and fresh white ground pepper, to taste
Freshly grated nutmeg

HOW TO MAKE THE ROCKFISH: Season both sides of the rockfish with salt and pepper and set aside.

Cut the shiitake mushrooms into ¼- to ½-inch slices. Tear the oyster mushrooms into manageable bite-size strips, and quarter the morels. Make sure both the oyster mushrooms and morels have been cleaned very well of any dirt. Combine all mushrooms in one container.

In a large sauté pan, melt 2 tablespoons of the unsalted butter over medium-high heat. Add half of the mushrooms and toss well to coat thoroughly. Add a little salt and pepper and stir frequently. Once the mushrooms begin to caramelize and become crisp on their edges (if the mushrooms begin to look dried out during this process, add more butter), add half of the shallots and garlic and sauté for 1 minute more. Add half of the thyme and deglaze and flambé the mushrooms with 1 ounce of the brandy. Adjust the seasoning to taste, remove from heat, and hold warm while repeating the same steps with the remaining mushrooms.

As the last batch of mushrooms is finishing, add the clarified butter (or vegetable oil) to a cast-iron skillet or nonstick sauté pan over medium-high heat. Place the seasoned rockfish, presentation side down, into the hot butter and allow a golden crust to form. Turn the fish once, cook for about 1 to 2 minutes more, and turn off the heat, leaving the fish in the pan.

HOW TO MAKE THE PUMPKIN SAUCE: Combine the wine and shallots in a heavy-bottomed saucepan and reduce by half. Add the pumpkin puree and stir together to combine completely. Slowly whisk in the heavy cream and allow the sauce to simmer over low heat for 8 to 10 minutes, or until slightly thickened, whisking frequently. Season the sauce with salt and pepper and strain through a

fine-mesh sieve. Keep warm until ready to serve or cool immediately and reheat over low heat when needed.

How to make the parsnip puree: Wash, peel, trim off the tops, and cut the parsnips into 1-inch pieces. Place the cut parsnips into a medium saucepot and allow cold water to run until water becomes clear. Cover the parsnips with cold water and bring to a boil over medium heat and reduce to a simmer. Cook until fork tender. Meanwhile, in a heavy-bottomed saucepot, bring the butter, cream, and rosemary to a simmer. Remove from heat, strain, and keep warm. Once the parsnips are tender, pass them through a food mill and, in small increments, add the rosemary-infused cream until the puree is firm (not runny). Season well with salt and a small amount of white pepper and nutmeg and serve hot.

How to plate: Lace a 1- to 2-ounce ladle of the pumpkin sauce directly in the middle of a warm plate and mold or pipe some parsnip puree in the center of the sauce. Prop the seared rockfish over the top of the parsnips and place a heaping mound of the warm mushroom salad on top of the fish, allowing it to cascade down into the sauce. Serve immediately.

MAKES 4 SERVINGS

"Yellow-eye rockfish are one of
the prettiest of Alaska's bottom-dwellers."

Pecan-Crusted Alaska Yellow-Eye Rockfish with Creamy Leeks and Lavender Honey-Roasted Root Vegetables

For the Rockfish
2 cups shelled and coarsely chopped pecans
½ cup all-purpose flour
4 5-ounce portions Alaska yellow-eye rockfish
Pinch kosher salt and fresh ground pepper, to taste
1 cup egg wash (1 egg plus 1 tablespoon water)
2 ounces clarified butter

For the Creamy Leeks
2 pounds fresh leeks, white and pale green portion only, root ends trimmed
¼ cup unsalted butter
1 large shallot, peeled with ends trimmed, finely sliced
1 teaspoon finely chopped fresh thyme
1 cup heavy cream
Pinch kosher salt and fresh ground pepper, to taste
Fresh ground nutmeg

For the Honey-Roasted Root Vegetables
½ pound golden beets
½ pound parsnips
½ pound carrots
½ pound rutabaga
1 tablespoon clarified butter
1 tablespoon peeled, trimmed, and finely minced shallot
Pinch kosher salt and fresh ground pepper, to taste
Lavender honey

HOW TO MAKE THE ROCKFISH: In a shallow pan, combine chopped nuts and half of the flour. (Note: Pecans are very high in fat and must be cut with the flour to prevent them from forming into sticky clumps; add more flour if needed.)

Season the rockfish on both sides with salt and pepper. Dredge the rockfish through the plain all-purpose flour, shaking off any excess. Next, dredge the rockfish through the egg wash, thoroughly coating both sides, and shake off the excess egg. Place the fish into the pecan/flour mixture and gently press the nut mixture onto both sides, coating well.

Heat enough clarified butter in a sauté pan to just cover the bottom of the pan over medium-low heat. Once hot (should not be smoking; remember, nuts burn easily), lay the crusted rockfish into the pan. Cook over medium heat, turning to cook both sides, until nuts are golden brown and the fish is just cooked through, about 2 to 3 minutes each side, depending on the thickness of the fish.

HOW TO MAKE THE CREAMY LEEKS: Split the leeks lengthwise and wash each layer to remove any dirt. Cut the leeks in half into 3- to 4-inch-long segments and thinly slice into ¼- to ⅛-inch-long strips; store in cool water until ready to use. Drain the leeks well, reserving about ¼ cup for garnishing, and heat the butter in a large sauté pan over a low flame. Add the leeks, shallot, and thyme to the pan and gently sauté, stirring frequently until tender. Add the cream to the leeks and continue to cook, stirring occasionally, until the mixture has thickened. Season to taste with salt, pepper, and nutmeg. Serve hot or cool immediately and gently reheat when ready to use.

How to make the honey-roasted root vegetables: Trim the tops and peel the beets, parsnips, carrots, and rutabaga, keeping all of the vegetables separate. Cut each vegetable into ½-inch rough-cut pieces and separately submerge in cold water. (Note: Make certain to allow water to run over each vegetable until the water runs clear. This removes excess starch and sugars.) Next, place the beets in a small saucepot and add enough cold water to cover them. Bring to a boil and reduce to a simmer until they become al dente (tender with a slight bite). Drain from hot water immediately and submerge in ice water until completely cool. Drain and store refrigerated until ready to use. Follow the same steps with the remaining vegetables. Once the vegetables have been par-cooked, all but the beets may be stored together. When ready to use, melt the butter in a nonstick sauté pan over medium-high heat. In batches, sauté the carrots, parsnips, and rutabaga until hot and their edges begin to turn golden brown, about 2 to 3 minutes. Add the beets and warm through. Quickly add the shallots, salt and pepper to taste, and drizzle with a little lavender honey. Remove from heat immediately and hold warm until ready to plate. Be careful not to overcook the root vegetables. They should be tender with a slight bite, not mushy.

How to plate: In a serving bowl, ladle a heaping portion of the creamy leeks in the center of the bowl and surround the leeks with a medley of the honey-roasted root vegetables. Place the hot pecan-crusted rockfish on the leeks, and garnish with a fresh chiffonade of leek, if desired, and serve immediately.

MAKES 4 SERVINGS

"Pat dry and season both sides of the fish with salt and a little pepper. The seasoning sticks better and the simple seasoning of salt and pepper brings out and accents the wonderful flavor of this fish. Keep the fish refrigerated. Once the fish has been seasoned, place it back in the refrigerator immediately until you are ready to cook. This assures the freshness of the yellow-eye is maintained."

Alaska Yellow-Eye Rockfish Puttanesca

For the Puttanesca Salsa (makes 2 cups)

2 medium heirloom tomatoes, quartered, seeded, and diced small
1/4 medium red onion, diced small
1/2 tablespoon minced garlic
Pinch kosher salt and fresh ground pepper, to taste
8 teaspoons red wine vinegar
3 teaspoons anchovy paste
1/2 cup extra-virgin olive oil
12 kalamata olives, pitted and diced small
2 tablespoons chopped capers, rinsed

For the Herb Crostini (makes 24–32 pieces)

1 baguette, multigrain or French
2 cups extra-virgin olive oil
1 cup finely chopped fresh Italian parsley
Pinch kosher salt and fresh ground pepper, to taste

For the Rockfish

8 3-ounce portions fresh Alaska yellow-eye rockfish
Pinch kosher salt and fresh ground pepper, to taste
2 ounces clarified butter
1 pound fresh baby arugula
2 cups fresh puttanesca salsa
24 herb crostini, 1/2 inch thick
8 slices pancetta, 1/4 inch thick, cooked crisp
1 tablespoon fresh basil, chiffonade (cut into long, thin strips)

HOW TO MAKE THE PUTTANESCA SALSA: Combine the tomatoes and onion, toss with the garlic, and season with salt and pepper. In a separate bowl, combine the vinegar and anchovy paste. Slowly drizzle 1/4 cup olive oil into the vinegar and anchovy mixture, whisking constantly, until slightly thickened (add more olive oil if needed). Next, add the kalamata olives and capers to the tomato and onion mixture. Drizzle in the vinegar and anchovy mixture and toss gently to just coat. Season with salt and pepper and serve slightly chilled or at room temperature.

HOW TO MAKE THE HERB CROSTINI: Preheat the oven to 400°F. Slice the baguette on a sharp bias, making 1/2-inch-thick slices. Place in a single layer on a baking sheet. With a basting brush, lightly coat the entire top of each slice of baguette with olive oil. Bake for 9 to 11 minutes or until the tops of the crostini are a beautiful golden brown. Remove from the oven and immediately sprinkle with the chopped Italian parsley, salt, and pepper. Cool at room temperature and store in an airtight container until needed.

HOW TO MAKE THE ROCKFISH: Season the rockfish on both sides with salt and pepper. In a cast-iron skillet or a nonstick sauté pan, heat enough clarified butter to just cover the bottom of the pan over medium-high heat. Sear the presentation side of the rockfish until a golden crust forms and immediately turn the fish over and turn off the heat, leaving the fish in the skillet.

In a mixing bowl, toss the baby arugula with a little of the puttanesca salsa and a little pepper.

HOW TO PLATE: Fan 3 pieces of crostini with their ends meeting in the center of a plate. Place a small mound of the dressed arugula on top of the ends of the crostini where they meet and tuck the crisp pancetta slice into the arugula so that it stands erect. Place the seared rockfish against the pancetta and mound with a heaping tablespoon of the puttanesca salsa. You may use more or less to your preference. Garnish with the fresh basil and a drizzle around the plate of the butter from the seared fish skillet. Serve immediately.

MAKES 8 SERVINGS

Sunchoke-Crusted Alaska Yellow-Eye Rockfish with Black Quinoa Cakes and Fennel Jam

For the Rockfish
1 large sunchoke (aka Jerusalem artichoke)
4 5-ounce portions fresh Alaska yellow-eye rockfish
Pinch kosher salt and fresh ground pepper, to taste
1 large egg, beaten well
1 tablespoon finely chopped fresh tarragon
4 tablespoons clarified butter (or vegetable oil)

For the Black Quinoa Cakes
1½ cups vegetable stock
½ teaspoon salt
1 cup black quinoa
1 small yellow onion, julienned
2 tablespoons unsalted butter
1 tablespoon minced garlic
Pinch kosher salt and fresh ground pepper, to taste
1 large egg, beaten well
4 tablespoons olive oil
2–4 tablespoons all-purpose flour

HOW TO MAKE THE SUNCHOKE-CRUSTED ROCKFISH: First, scrub the sunchoke well with a vegetable brush under cold running water to remove all dirt from its surface. Leave the sunchoke whole or cut into quarters or halves, depending on the width of your fish. On a Japanese mandoline, or with a sharp knife, cut paper-thin slices of sunchoke and immediately store in cold lemon water until ready to use to prevent oxidation.

Pat the rockfish portions dry with a paper towel and season both sides with salt and pepper. With a basting brush, lightly coat the presentation side of the rockfish with the beaten egg.

Drain and pat dry the sunchoke slices and carefully create a shingled "crust" on the egg-washed side of the rockfish. Make sure the slices overlap one another in order to cover the entire top surface area of the fish. You may need to partially coat the sunchoke slices in order for them to stick together if they are thicker pieces. Sprinkle the shingled sunchoke slices with the chopped tarragon.

In a nonstick skillet, heat the clarified butter or oil over medium-high heat. Using both hands to keep the sunchoke shingles in place, carefully place the sunchoke side of the rockfish into the hot pan. Turn the heat down to medium. Once the edges of the sunchokes start to turn golden brown, gently turn the fish over to finish cooking, about 3 to 5 minutes, depending on the thickness of the fish. Remove from heat and reserve.

HOW TO MAKE THE BLACK QUINOA CAKES: Preheat oven to 375°F. In a medium heavy-bottomed saucepot, bring the vegetable stock and ½ teaspoon salt to a boil. Meanwhile, wash the quinoa in 3 changes of hot water in a bowl, draining well through a fine-mesh sieve. Stir the quinoa into the boiling stock, return to a boil, and then simmer over low heat, covered, until the quinoa has absorbed all of the stock and is tender, about 15 to 20 minutes. Remove from heat and let stand, covered, 5 minutes. Transfer to a large bowl and cool refrigerated, stirring occasionally, about 10 minutes.

While the quinoa is cooking, sauté the onion over medium heat in a sauté pan with the butter until the onion begins to develop a beautiful golden color. Add the garlic and cook for about 5 minutes. Remove from heat, season with salt and pepper, and set aside. Once the quinoa has cooled, stir in the caramelized onions and season accordingly. Stir in the beaten egg, 2 tablespoons olive oil, and enough flour to allow the mixture to just stick together. Add more oil and flour if needed.

Line a baking sheet with plastic wrap and lightly brush with oil. Lightly oil a ½-cup dry-ingredient measuring cup and firmly pack enough quinoa into the cup to fill it. Unmold onto the baking sheet and repeat the process, making 3 more quinoa cakes, brushing the cup with oil each time. Chill the cakes, uncovered, at least 15 minutes or overnight (cover if stored overnight). Next, heat 2 tablespoons of oil or clarified butter in a nonstick skillet over medium heat until it ripples. Carefully add the quinoa cakes and cook, turning once, until crisp and golden brown on each side. Transfer back to baking sheet and warm in preheated oven for 5 to 8 minutes.

HOW TO MAKE THE FENNEL JAM: Remove the stalks and fronds from the fennel bulb and cut the bulb in half from top to bottom. Cut out and discard the core from the bulb and slice about ¼ inch thick on a mandoline (or using a sharp knife). Melt the butter with the olive oil in a small saucepot over medium-high heat. Add the sliced fennel, onion, and shallot and cook, stirring frequently. Once color begins to develop on the vegetables, turn heat to low and continue to cook until the mixture becomes tender and is beautifully caramelized. Add 2 tablespoons of the white balsamic vinegar to deglaze the pan, careful to not breathe in the vinegar fumes, and turn the

For the Fennel Jam
1 medium fennel bulb
2 tablespoons unsalted butter
2 tablespoons extra-virgin olive oil
½ medium sweet Spanish onion, julienned
1 medium shallot, peeled, ends trimmed, finely sliced
2–4 tablespoons white balsamic vinegar
Pinch kosher salt and fresh ground pepper, to taste

heat to very low, stirring frequently until the vinegar reduces slightly and its sugars coat the fennel-onion mixture, about 1 to 2 minutes. Remove from heat and taste the "jam." Season with salt and pepper, and if desired, add more white balsamic vinegar for your own flavor preference. Serve immediately or at room temperature.

HOW TO PLATE: Remove the rockfish from the pan and serve immediately with the hot black quinoa cake and a large spoonful of fennel jam. Garnish with tender fronds of fennel, if desired.

MAKES 4 SERVINGS

"One day while I was experimenting with Alaska yellow-eye rockfish, I wanted to try it without any sauces, special preparation, or seasonings in order to truly understand the unique flavor of this particular species. I went over to my brother and sister-in-law's house and simply salted and lightly peppered the yellow-eye and seared it in extra-virgin olive oil. Growing up in Alaska, inevitably you end up eating a lot of over-cooked fish that can really turn you off. That has been the case with my brother and his wife. I made certain to very quickly sear one side and then turn off the heat once I turned the fish over and let it finish cooking with carry-over heat. They loved it and made quick work of finishing all of the fillets I had prepared. It is always such a pleasure to have someone eat something they have previously excluded from their food repertoire and introduce it in such a way that they gain a whole new outlook on the product."

"Alaska yellow-eye is not an extremely thick fish, and it cooks very quickly. I recommend making sure the pan the rockfish will be cooked in is nice and hot, and once the first side of the fish has a little color on it, turn, turn off the heat, and allow the residual heat from the pan to finish cooking the fish. This will maintain its succulent moisture every time."

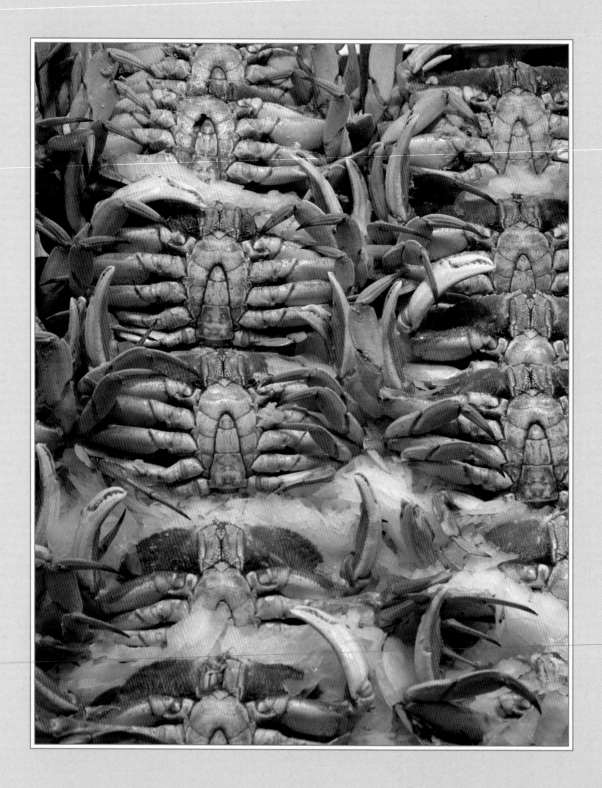

"I love Dungeness crab for its pristine and sweet flavor, for the bounty of harvest in Alaska and the Northwest, and for the versatility it represents."

—Executive Chef Jason Wilson

Chapter 14

DUNGENESS CRAB

EXECUTIVE CHEF JASON WILSON—CRUSH

*D*ungeness crab, named after a small fishing village on the Strait of Juan de Fuca in Washington State, have been harvested commercially since the late 1800s. They range from central California to the Gulf of Alaska and have long been part of the Northwest's seafood heritage.

Dungeness crab are caught in circular steel traps called "pots" weighing anywhere from 60 to 125 pounds. Only male crabs measuring at least 6½ inches across the shell may be harvested. Small males and all females are returned alive to the sea. The average crabber fishes 250 to 300 pots, in depths ranging from 30 to 180 feet of water.

Chef Jason Wilson's ingredient-driven modern American cuisine has garnered him and his restaurant, Crush, local and national accolades, including a 2006 "Best New Chef" award from *Food and Wine*. And his vivacious personality has led to a number of television appearances and international food events.

As a graduate of the California Culinary Academy in San Francisco, Chef Wilson has spent time in some of the most influential kitchens in San Francisco, such as Flying Saucer, Aqua, and Stars. He has also traveled and cooked extensively throughout Southeast Asia and Europe, including years at Singapore Stars and apprenticeships in Paris and Tain l'Hermitage. Together with Nicole Wilson, he created Crush, one of Seattle's finest upscale restaurants, which manages to combine ambitious cuisine with a laid-back atmosphere. ✑

"When removing crabmeat from the shells, I often use a black light, as the shells illuminate intensely under this light. Try it, and you'll be surprised how many pieces of shell you'll find in your crabmeat."

Dungeness Crab Fritters with Pistou Dipping Sauce

HOW TO MAKE THE CRAB FRITTERS: In a stainless steel saucepot on medium heat, simmer the leeks and shallots in the cream for 6 minutes. Add the chili flakes, paprika, and lemon, and allow 5 minutes to cool. Pour the mixture into a stainless steel mixing bowl and fold in the crabmeat, parsley, and mint. Add the eggs, one by one, followed by the egg yolk. Stir well to combine. Next, add the baking powder, flour, salt, and pepper, and mix well. Allow 5 minutes to rest, then fry in hot (360°F) canola oil until crisp. (Note: These fritters are basically a leavened crab cake and make for an excellent starter course.)

HOW TO MAKE THE PISTOU DIPPING SAUCE: Start by blanching the parsley, basil, tarragon, and garlic. This is acheived by submerging them in salted boiling water for 30 seconds, removing them from the water, and immediately plunging them in icewater to stop the cooking process. When cold, remove from water and remove excess moisture by pressing with paper towel. Chop the herbs and garlic.

Next, puree the parsley, basil, and tarragon with the garlic. Add the olive oil and salt, and puree until smooth. Add the preserved lemon, pistachios, gum, and egg yolk, and puree until smooth and emulsified.

HOW TO PLATE: Plate the fritters on a platter and serve warm with a side of pistou dipping sauce.

MAKES 6–8 SERVINGS

For the Crab Fritters
1 medium leek, finely chopped
3 tablespoons finely chopped shallots
1 cup heavy cream
1 tablespoon red pepper chili flakes
1/2 teaspoon smoked paprika
2 tablespoons finely chopped preserved lemon
1 pound fresh Dungeness crabmeat
1 tablespoon chopped fresh parsley
1 tablespoon chopped fresh mint
2 whole eggs
1 egg yolk
1/2 teaspoon baking powder
1/2 cup flour
1 tablespoon kosher salt
1/2 teaspoon black pepper
Canola oil, for frying

For the Pistou Dipping Sauce (makes 12 ounces)
1/2 bunch fresh parsley
1 bunch fresh basil
1/2 bunch fresh tarragon
3 ounces garlic
7 ounces olive oil
1 ounce kosher salt
3 ounces finely diced preserved lemon
3 ounces pistachios
1/8 ounce xanthan gum (available at health food stores or in the baking section of fine grocery stores)
1 egg yolk

Warm Dungeness Crab Salad with Cucumber Vinaigrette

For the Crab Salad
¼ cup finely diced leeks
¼ cup finely diced shallots
1 pint heavy cream
3 pounds fresh Dungeness
    crabmeat
1 teaspoon kosher salt
1 tablespoon lemon zest
2 tablespoons finely
    chopped fresh Italian
    parsley
1 tablespoon finely chopped
    fresh mint
1 tablespoon finely chopped
    fresh tarragon
3 tablespoons crème fraiche

For the Cucumber
Vinaigrette
1 English cucumber, peeled
    and seeded
3 tablespoons fresh lemon
    juice
⅓ cup extra-virgin olive oil
2 tablespoons kosher salt
10 fresh mint leaves
1 teaspoon minced fresh
    chives
Blanched sea beans, for
    garnish
Shaved radishes, for garnish
Shaved cucumber, for
    garnish
Minced chives, for garnish

HOW TO MAKE THE CRAB SALAD: In a stainless steel saucepot over medium heat, simmer the leeks and shallots in the cream for 20 minutes, or until the mixture is reduced by half. Drain the crabmeat of any liquid/water and pour the warm mixture over the crabmeat. Season with salt, and add the lemon zest, parsley, mint, tarragon, and crème fraiche. Toss gently to combine.

HOW TO MAKE THE CUCUMBER VINAIGRETTE: Puree the cucumber, lemon juice, olive oil, salt, mint, and chives until blended. Strain the mixture through a fine-mesh strainer and reserve until ready to use.

HOW TO PLATE: Warm the crab slightly in the oven before spooning into ring molds. Place one mold in the center of each plate and remove the ring. Drizzle the salad with the cucumber vinaigrette and garnish with sea beans, shaved radishes, cucumber, and chives.

MAKES 4 SERVINGS

"Not long ago, I was in Sitka, Alaska, with four clients eager to do some king salmon fishing. Unfortunately, the weather was far too stormy to do the guided fishing we intended, so we dropped some crab pots. We harvested twenty-four crabs and brought them back to the boat we were staying on. I spent hours boiling the crab in seawater and preparing them on the top deck while gazing out into the Sitka Sound as the weather began to clear. During the following days of epic salmon fishing, we feasted on the crab during breakfast, lunch, and dinner. To this day, my favorite place to feast on Dungeness crab is in Sitka."

Dungeness Crab and Leek Gratin with Sweet Pork Crumbs

HOW TO MAKE THE CRAB AND LEEK GRATIN: In a stainless steel saucepot over medium heat, add the duck fat and cream. Add the leeks, garlic, and lemon zest and simmer until reduced by half. Add the thyme and parsley, and simmer 15 minutes. Add the salt and fold in the crabmeat. In a separate pan, render the bacon until crispy. Add the brown sugar and cook an additional 4 minutes on medium heat until the sugar melts. Place the warm mixture into a casserole dish and top with the bread crumbs and bacon bits. Bake in a pre-heated oven at 400°F for 20 minutes. Allow 5 minutes to rest.

HOW TO PLATE: Serve "family-style" by placing the casserole dish in the middle of the table for all to enjoy. (Note: the casserole also makes a fantastic breakfast item with poached eggs.)

MAKES 6 SERVINGS

- ½ cup clean duck fat (or substitute with butter)
- ½ cup heavy cream
- 2 leeks, sliced in rings ¼ inch thick and soaked in warm water
- 2 cloves garlic
- 2 tablespoons lemon zest
- ⅓ bunch fresh thyme, sprigs removed and chopped fine
- 2 tablespoons chopped fresh parsley
- 2 tablespoons sea salt
- 2 pounds fresh Dungeness crabmeat
- ⅓ pound country bacon, chopped fine
- 3 tablespoons brown sugar
- ½ cup brioche bread crumbs, whites only, lightly toasted

> "True fact that Dungeness crabmeat is readily available in seafood markets and grocery stores, but always purchase live when possible. Live crab cooked in salted water will taste like the ocean and will yield a far superior flavor."

Spiced Dungeness Crab with Melon Soup

For the Spiced Crab

1 red jalapeño pepper, finely
  minced
3 cloves garlic, finely
  chopped
2 shallots, finely chopped
1/2 teaspoon smoked paprika
1/2 teaspoon ground fennel
2 tablespoons kosher salt
1/2 teaspoon ground black
  pepper
2 tablespoons lemon juice
3 tablespoons olive oil
1/4 bunch mint, chopped fine
1/2 tablespoon ground red
  chili flakes
1/2 tablespoon brown sugar
1 pound Dungeness
  crabmeat

For the Melon Soup

1 1/2 pounds canary melon,
  cleaned, seeded, and
  chopped
1/4 bunch fresh mint
2 ounces extra-virgin olive oil
1 ounce sea salt
1/8 ounce fresh jalapeño
10–12 cups vegetable stock

HOW TO MAKE THE SPICED CRAB: In a large bowl, combine the jalapeño, garlic, shallots, smoked paprika, fennel, salt, pepper, lemon juice, olive oil, mint, chili flakes, and brown sugar. Whisk to incorporate. Add the Dungeness crabmeat, toss, and let marinate for 45 minutes.

HOW TO MAKE THE MELON SOUP: Puree the melon with the mint, olive oil, sea salt, jalapeño, and vegetable stock. When pureed, pass through a soup strainer and chill.

HOW TO PLATE: Divide the spiced crab among individual serving plates and ladle the soup around the crab. Garnish with a couple endive leaves.

MAKES 6 SERVINGS

WE PACK FISH TO GO FOR 48 HOURS

ALL CRAB NO EXTRA CH

"Don't discard those crab shells. They make a very good soup base or stock for bisques. Overcooking the shells, however, can lead to an ammonia-like flavor and aroma. It's best to use a pressure cooker to achieve a great flavored stock or soup base, and it will only need to cook for 15 minutes."

Dungeness Crab Summer Succotash

HOW TO MAKE THE DUNGENESS CRAB STOCK: In a stainless steel pressure cooker on medium-high heat, sweat the shallots, celery, garlic, leek, parsley, and basil in olive oil. Add the salt, bay leaves, brandy, and water and let simmer until fragrant, about 8 minutes. Add the remaining ingredients, close the lid, and cook at full pressure, high temperature for 15 minutes. Allow 10 minutes for presure cooker to relax. Strain stock through a strainer and reserve refrigerated.

HOW TO MAKE THE SUMMER SUCCOTASH: In a stainless steel sauté pan on medium-high heat, add the olive oil. When hot, add the green and yellow zucchini and sauté until just tender. Spoon onto a parchment-lined sheet pan to cool. Repeat the process with the bell peppers and onions, adding more olive oil if necessary. Next, sauté the corn in butter, and let cool with the other vegetables.

In the same pan, simmer the garlic, Dungeness crab stock (or store-bought chicken stock), and tomato juice until reduced by half. Reduce heat to low and fold in the sautéed vegetables. Cook over low heat for 3 minutes. Fold in the crabmeat, blanched fava beans, chives, and parsley. Season with salt.

HOW TO PLATE: Transfer the succotash to a serving platter and serve as a side dish with grilled or roasted fish, or as a lunch item with fresh arugula and poached eggs.

MAKES 6 SERVINGS

For the Dungeness Crab Stock*
2 shallots, chopped small
2 celery ribs, sliced thin
2 cloves garlic
1 large leek, green removed, sliced thin
1/4 bunch fresh Italian flatleaf parlsey
1/4 bunch fresh basil
3 tablespoons olive oil
2 tablespoons kosher salt
2 bay leaves
1/4 cup brandy
1 pint water
2 pounds fresh Dungeness crab shells and bodies
1 quart chicken stock
3 tablespoons tomato juice
*For this recipe, the Dungeness crab stock can be replaced with canned or boxed chicken stock.

For the Dungeness Crab Succotash
3 ounces olive oil
1/4 cup seeded and small-diced green zucchini
1/4 cup seeded and small-diced yellow zucchini
1/4 cup seeded and small-diced red bell peppers
1/4 cup seeded and small-diced yellow bell peppers
2 tablespoons small-diced red onion
1 pound white corn kernels
2 ounces unsalted butter
1 teaspoon finely diced garlic
2 cups Dungeness crab stock
4 ounces tomato juice
1 pound fresh Dungeness crabmeat
1/2 pound fava beans, blanched
1/4 bunch chopped fresh chives
1/4 bunch chopped fresh parsley
Pinch kosher salt, to taste

"It is imperative that we support and buy from purveyors who have a respect for the ocean."

—Executive Chef Leonardo Curti

Chapter 15

LITTLENECK "STEAMER" CLAMS

EXECUTIVE CHEF LEONARDO CURTI—TRATTORIA GRAPPOLO

*L*ittleneck or "steamer" clams are the sweetest-tasting and most tender of the clams. They have shells measuring less than 2 inches across and are often eaten raw or steamed, hence the nickname "steamers." Due to increased fishing and various environmental hazards, many littlenecks, and other clams, are now being farmed, offering a better alternative to wild-caught clams.

> "I love the freshness, taste, and simplicity of clams. They're the perfect seafood because they pair with almost everything."

Farmed clams start out in a hatchery where they are fed continuously and grow rapidly. Once the clams grow to sufficient size, they are taken out to floating nursery rafts. After they grow further, they are shipped to another growing area where they are planted with net panels. The clams work their way through the mesh net and into the sand where they are protected from predators. Once they reach market size, the clams are dug and bagged, just like in the wild, and suspended from wet storage rafts to purge the sand until they are sold.

Chef Leonardo Curti is the executive chef and coproprietor at the acclaimed Trattoria Grappolo bistro in Santa Ynez, California. Born in Calabria, Italy, Chef Curti learned his culinary skills in Tuscany before relocating to Los Angeles, where he worked as a chef at Cicada Restaurant and founded Pane Caldo in Beverly Hills. Chef Curti's gastronomic journey then led him to Aspen where he joined the legendary Farfalla restaurant. In 1997 he opened Trattoria Grappolo in Santa Ynez and hasn't looked back.

Today, the casual bistro continues to serve authentic, traditional Italian fare for lunch and dinner. Aside from the restaurant, Chef Curti runs a full catering company and teaches private cooking classes. He also launched a new line of pasta sauces.

Fresh "Steamer" Clam Omelet

¼ cup extra-virgin olive oil
2 garlic cloves, minced
1 cup freshly shelled
    littleneck "steamer" clams,
    juice reserved
1 tablespoon chopped fresh
    Italian parsley
¼ cup dry white wine
Pinch salt and pepper, to
    taste
6 eggs
¼ cup milk

How to make the omelet: In a 10- to 12-inch nonstick pan over medium-high heat, add the olive oil and garlic, cooking for about 2 minutes. Add the clams, clam juice, parsley, white wine, and salt and pepper. Allow the alcohol to evaporate, cooking for a couple minutes. In a bowl, whisk the eggs and milk together, and add to the skillet, reducing the heat to medium. Cook for about 4 minutes or until golden on the bottom. Flip the omelet over and brown the other side. Serve immediately.

MAKES 2–4 SERVINGS

Toasted Couscous with Littleneck "Steamer" Clams

TO MAKE THE COUSCOUS: Cook the couscous according to the package directions.

TO MAKE THE CLAM SAUCE: In a large saucepan over medium-high heat, add the oil and garlic. Cook for about 1 minute. Add the clams and cover. Add the wine and allow for the alcohol to evaporate. Add the clam juice, salt and pepper, crushed red pepper, and tomatoes, arugula, and parsley. Continue to cook for about 4 minutes.

HOW TO PLATE: When the couscous is finished cooking, drain and add to the clam sauce. Toss and serve immediately in individual serving bowls.

MAKES 4 SERVINGS

1 package couscous
¼ cup olive oil
3 garlic cloves, smashed
2 pounds live littleneck "steamer" clams
¼ cup white wine
½ cup clam juice
Pinch salt and pepper, to taste
Pinch crushed red pepper
½ cup cherry tomatoes
½ cup fresh arugula
2 tablespoons chopped fresh Italian parsley

"When cooking clams with olive oil over a heat source, make sure your clams are dry. This will help to reduce the oil from 'popping' and splattering. Wet clams and hot oil don't mix."

Sautéed "Steamer" Clams

1/4 cup extra-virgin olive oil
4 garlic cloves, crushed
2 pounds live littleneck "steamer" clams
1/2 cup dry white wine
2 tablespoons finely chopped fresh Italian parsley
Pinch salt and pepper, to taste
1 cup clam juice
Pinch crushed red pepper
1/2 lemon
Toasted country bread

To MAKE THE CLAMS: In a large skillet over medium-high heat, add the olive oil and crushed garlic. Cook for about 1 minute. Add the clams and cover the skillet with a lid to allow the clams to open. Once the clams are open, add the white wine and allow the wine to evaporate, about 2 minutes. Add the Italian parsley, salt and pepper to taste, clam juice, and the crushed red pepper. Continue to cook for about 5 minutes, raising the heat to high.

How TO PLATE: Divide the clams in individual serving bowls. Discard any unopen clams. Pour the remaining juice from the skillet over the clams. Finish each bowl with a squeeze of fresh lemon juice. Serve with a side of toasted country bread.

MAKES 2–4 SERVINGS

"When I was a young boy growing up in Italy, I would snorkel every morning in the Ionian Sea. Next to where I'd enter the water, there were bags full with live clams. The owners of Lidos—a small, family-run seaside eatery—stored their clams here, and when a customer ordered a clam dish, the owners would rush to the water's edge and retrieve one of their bags. Because I loved the taste of clams, my snorkeling outings soon became covert collecting missions, where I'd collect just enough so I could rush down the beach to cook them over an open fire with friends."

"When cooking with wild clams, allow them to soak for at least an hour so they can purge the sand. Otherwise, you'll be eating gritty clams. I prefer farm-raised clams, because they've already been purged of sand."

"Steamer" Clam and Ricotta Ravioli

HOW TO MAKE THE RICOTTA RAVIOLI: Lay the egg roll skins in a line. In the middle of each egg roll skin, add 1 tablespoon ricotta cheese. Brush the sides of each egg roll skin with the egg wash. Fold and seal each egg roll skin to make a triangle. Next, bring 4 quarts of salted water to a boil. When the clam sauce is almost finished cooking, add the raviolis, 4 or 5 at a time, to the boiling water. Let cook for about 2 minutes.

HOW TO MAKE THE CLAM SAUCE: In a large skillet over medium-high heat, heat the oil. Add the garlic and cook for about 1 minute. Add the clams and allow them to open. Add the white wine, salt and pepper, and the parsley and cook for another 5 minutes. Add the zucchini, carrots, and clam juice. Remove from heat as soon as all the clams are open. Discard any unopen clams.

HOW TO PLATE: Using a sieve or slotted spoon, scoop out the raviolis from the boiling water and arrange on individual serving plates. Pour the clam sauce over the raviolis and divide the cooked clams in the shell on each plate. Serve immediately.

MAKES 4 SERVINGS

For the Ricotta Ravioli
1 package large egg roll skins
2 cups fresh ricotta cheese
1 egg, beaten

For the Clam Sauce
$1/4$ cup extra-virgin olive oil
2 garlic cloves, crushed
1 pound littleneck "steamer" clams
$1/4$ cup dry white wine
Pinch salt and pepper, to taste
1 tablespoon chopped fresh Italian parsley
1 small zucchini, julienned
1 small carrot, julienned
$1/4$ cup clam juice

> "Always discard any unopened clams after cooking. The reason they didn't open is because they were already dead or the shells are filled with sand."

Littleneck "Steamer" Clam Pizza with Tomato

For the Sauce (makes 2 cups)
2 cups Italian tomato puree
2 tablespoons extra-virgin olive oil
Dash dried oregano
1 clove garlic, peeled and smashed
Pinch sea salt, to taste

For the Dough
1 package dry active yeast
2 cups Italian natural spring water (bottled and still, such as Sole)
2 teaspoons sea salt
6 cups all-purpose Italian flour
2 tablespooons extra-virgin olive oil

For the Clams
2–3 cloves garlic, crushed
Pinch sea salt and black pepper, to taste
1 cup white wine
2 pounds live "steamer" clams
6–8 fresh basil leaves
½ tablespoon dried oregano
Extra-virgin olive oil

HOW TO MAKE THE SAUCE: In a blender, add all of the ingredients and puree until combined. Store in refrigerator until ready to use.

HOW TO MAKE THE DOUGH: In an electric mixer with the dough hook attached, stir yeast and lukewarm water until combined. Add salt and flour until dough begins to form and is not sticky, about 10 to 12 minutes. Place dough in a bowl that has been lightly coated with oil. Coat the entire dough ball with oil as well. Cover bowl with plastic wrap and let dough rise in a warm place for about 1 hour. Remove dough from bowl and place on a smooth working surface. Divide the dough into 6 balls, about 6 to 7 ounces each. Place each dough ball on a lightly floured surface and cover with a towel. Let rise about 45 minutes. Makes 6 dough balls. Store extra dough balls by simply freezing in plastic wrap.

Dust a smooth working surface with flour. Place pizza dough ball in the center. Flatten the dough into a disc shape with your fingers. Next, roll the dough with a rolling pin until it is thin and reaches a diameter of 10 inches. Spoon the sauce evenly over the top; set aside.

HOW TO MAKE THE CLAMS: In a large pot over medium-high heat, bring the garlic, salt, pepper, and wine to a boil. Add the clams and cook until they open. Remove from heat, drain, and let cool. Discard any unopen clams. Remove the meat from the shells, reserving 4 or 5 clams in their shells. Arrange all the clams on top of the pizza. Place the pizza in a wood-fired oven, away from the fire, and let bake several minutes. Turn the pizza 180 degrees and continue baking another few minutes or until crust is golden brown. (Note: if using a conventional oven, cook pizza at 450°F on a preheated pizza stone on the middle oven rack.)

HOW TO PLATE: Remove pizza from the oven. Sprinkle with basil leaves and oregano and drizzle with olive oil.

MAKES 1 10-INCH PIZZA

"Octopus in North America comes in many different sizes and stages of preparation that help in being versatile with recipe creating. Octopus in most seafood markets is relatively inexpensive—sometimes as little as $2 a pound. You can get baby octopus that can be treated like calamari with quick cooking times or larger jumbo octopus up to 10 pounds that lend better to braising. The larger octopus can be bought already cleaned and cooked, such as tako in sushi markets, and simply need to be marinated or grilled."

—Executive Chef Shannon Galusha

Chapter 16

PACIFIC OCTOPUS

EXECUTIVE CHEF SHANNON GALUSHA—BASTILLE CAFÉ & BAR

The Pacific octopus is a large cephalopod found in the coastal North Pacific, usually at a depth of around 200 feet. It can, however, live in much shallower or much deeper waters. Adults usually weigh around 33 pounds with an arm span of up to 14 feet.

The Pacific octopus is distinguished from other species by its sheer size, although it's the smaller-size octopus (or young octopus) commonly used in the kitchen. The mantle of the octopus is spherical in shape and contains most of the animal's major organs. The skin of the octopus is somewhat smooth, and by contracting or expanding tiny pigments, an octopus can change the color of its skin, giving it the ability to blend into the environment.

A native of the Pacific Northwest, Chef Shannon Galusha applies his philosophy of "eliminating the unnecessary to obtain simplicity," resulting in exquisite culinary magic at Bastille Café & Bar. Chef Galusha's cuisine is inspired by the seasonal, prolific bounty of seafood, artisan products, and local farmers from the region.

Chef Galusha polished his culinary skills at the New England Culinary Institute, and upon graduating, he took on residency for three years at the world-renowned French Laundry in Yountville, California. He went on to work with various chefs across Europe, including two-star Michelin chef Michel Rostand. His impressive local résumé includes serving as executive sous-chef at Fullers in the Seattle Sheraton, executive sous-chef at Campagne and Café Campagne, executive chef at 727 Pine (formerly in the Seattle Grand Hyatt), and chef/partner at Veil Restaurant.

"Always select fresh seafood whenever possible. Tell your fish monger what you are planning to do with the seafood. Often they can perform difficult tasks such as removing parts like beaks, eyeballs, or ink sacs, cleaning the product, or something as simple as helping you know how much to buy for your preparation."

Grilled Octopus with Argon Oil, Marinated Chickpeas, and Harissa

HOW TO MAKE THE HARISSA: In a pan over medium heat, toast the chilis de arbole, ancho chilis, and chilis negro. When the chilis are nice and toasted, remove from heat. When cool to the touch, remove the chili stems and seeds. Allow to cool completely. When cool, add the clean pods to a spice grinder and grind to a powder. Next, add the cumin, coriander, smoked paprika, and sea salt.

HOW TO MAKE THE OCTOPUS: Place the octopus in a heavy-bottomed pot and cover with white wine. Add in the zest from 1 lemon and a crushed garlic clove. Bring the octopus to a simmer and cook for about 2 hours, or just until the tentacles are tender. Remove from the heat and, once cooled, remove from the liquid. Marinate only the tentacles with 3 to 4 tablespoons of the harissa spice and ¼ cup of olive oil for at least 30 minutes. Discard the hood. Grill the marinated tentacles over high heat until just warm and charred.

HOW TO MAKE THE MARINATED CHICKPEAS: Place half of the chickpeas in a blender with 1 cup olive oil, the juice from 1 lemon, and 1 or 2 garlic cloves, and puree until smooth and runny. Adjust the seasoning with sea salt. If the consistency is not runny, simply add some water.

Marinate the second half of the chickpeas with the ¼ cup argon oil, lemon juice, harissa spice, and crushed garlic, to taste.

HOW TO PLATE: Arrange the puree and marinated chickpeas on a large serving platter. Top with the grilled tentacles and serve immediately.

MAKES 4 SERVINGS

- 4 chilis de arbole, whole and dried
- 4 ancho chilis, whole and dried
- 4 chilis negro, whole and dried
- 1 teaspoon ground cumin
- 1 teaspoon ground coriander
- 1 tablespoon smoked paprika
- ¼ teaspoon sea salt
- 2½ pounds young octopus, cleaned with beak removed
- 1 quart dry white wine
- 2 lemons, 1 zested and 1 juiced
- 3 garlic cloves, crushed, divided
- 1¼ cups extra-virgin olive oil, divided
- 4 cups braised chickpeas
- ¼ cup argon oil

Octopus with Crispy Chorizo, Juarez Vinaigrette, and Butter Lettuce

8 ounces chorizo
1 cup salad oil, divided
6 ounces Juarez vinegar
1 tablespoon dijon mustard
2½ pounds young octopus,
    cleaned with beak
    removed
1 quart dry white wine
1 lemon, zested
1 garlic clove, crushed
1 tablespoon smoked paprika
¼ cup extra-virgin olive oil
4 heads of red butter lettuce
    or bibb, outer leaves
    removed, using only the
    light crisp inner leaves

HOW TO MAKE THE CRISPY CHORIZO: Peel the casing off the chorizo, slice thinly, then puree in a food processor with half the salad oil. Cook the pureed chorizo over medium heat until it becomes crisp like bacon. Remove from heat and keep warm.

HOW TO MAKE THE VINAIGRETTE: Combine the Juarez vinegar, mustard, and remaining salad oil in a blender and puree. Adjust the seasoning.

HOW TO MAKE THE OCTOPUS: Place the cleaned octopus in a heavy-bottomed pot and cover with white wine. Add in the lemon zest and crushed garlic clove. Bring the octopus to a simmer, and braise for about 2 hours, or until just tender. Remove from heat and, once cooled, remove the octopus from the liquid. Next, marinate only the octopus tentacles with the smoked paprika and the olive oil, and discard the hood. Keep the tentacles warm until ready to serve.

HOW TO PLATE: In a salad bowl, toss the marinated octopus with the chorizo. In a separate bowl, dress the cleaned lettuces and adjust seasoning. Stack the lettuce into a cup shape and top with the octopus. Garnish with a drizzle of the leftover chorizo oil from the bottom of the bowl.

MAKES 4 TO 5 SALADS

"When braising octopus in wine, use less-expensive or value-priced wines. Unlike braising meat or poultry, the liquid left over cannot be used and should be discarded."

"I use wild and local fresh fish whenever possible, as there is no need for frozen fish. I also see no reason to have our local dollars going overseas. If the fish isn't delivered by the fisherman through the back door with a handshake, it won't make it on my menus."

"Cork-Braised" Octopus and Orecchiette Pasta with Broccoli Rabe and Pine Nuts

How to make the octopus tentacles: Place the octopus tentacles in a pot and add the red wine. Add the bay leaves, peppercorns, the wine corks, and three of the chilis. Chop the fourth chili finely and reserve. Cover the pot and simmer, stirring the tentacles every 20 minutes, until tender. This will take about 1 hour. Let the tentacles cool in the liquid, then remove and slice into bite-size pieces or coins.

How to make the pasta: Cook the pasta al dente, according to package directions. When cooked, drain and toss with a light coating of olive oil.

How to make the broccoli rabe: Heat the remainder of the olive oil in a large pan. Add the rapini and sauté in the oil. Next add the reserved chopped chili, followed by the octopus slices, and then the cooked pasta. Toss well, adjust the seasoning with sea salt, and squeeze some fresh lemon juice over all.

How to plate: Divide among individual serving plates, and garnish with the fresh marjoram and pine nuts.

MAKES 4 SERVINGS

3–5 pounds of octopus tentacles, cleaned
4 cups red wine
6 bay leaves
10 peppercorns
15 wine corks
4 arbol chilis, divided
8 ounces orecchiette pasta
$1/2$ cup extra-virgin olive oil, divided
1 bunch broccoli rabe or rapini, stems removed and washed
Pinch sea salt, to taste
1 fresh lemon
4 tablespoons fresh marjoram leaves
$1/4$ cup pine nuts, toasted

"Cold octopus can be very chewy or rubbery. When serving larger octopus, like tako, always try to slice it thin, which helps reduce the toughness."

Pickled Octopus with Grilled Ramps, Fava Beans, and Toasted Bread

For the Octopus
2½ pounds octopus
6–8 tablespoons water
4 bunches fresh thyme
4 garlic cloves, crushed
Pinch sea salt, to taste
6 ounces extra-virgin
    olive oil
6 ounces white wine
    vinegar

For the Ramps
½ pound ramps,
    scallions, or baby
    leeks
Ice water, as needed
4 ounces water
4 ounces white wine
    vinegar
1 tablespoon white
    sugar
1 tablespoon pickling
    spice
1 baguette
2 tablespoons olive oil
Pinch sea salt

For the Fava Beans
½ pound fava beans

HOW TO MAKE THE OCTOPUS: Prepare and wash the octopus by removing the beak, ink sac, and eyes. Wash the octopus to remove any sand. Place the head and tentacles in a pan with 6 to 8 tablespoons of water. Cover and simmer for 1 hour to 1 hour 15 minutes, until octopus is tender. Remove the octopus from the liquid and let cool. Dice the octopus into bite-size pieces. Toss the octopus with the fresh thyme and crushed garlic, and season with sea salt. Completely cover the octopus with olive oil and vinegar and refrigerate for up to 2 weeks as a preserve, or just lightly coat with the olive oil and vinegar if you are serving immediately.

HOW TO MAKE THE RAMPS AND TOASTED BREAD: Set a large pot of water to boil. Wash the ramps to remove any dirt, separate the stem from the leaf, and remove the root. Blanch the stems for 2 minutes and cool in ice water. Combine the water, vinegar, sugar, and pickling spice and bring to a simmer. Strain out the pickling spice, cover the ramp stems, and allow to marinate for at least 1 hour. Slice the baguette thinly on a bias. Lightly brush both the bread and the ramp tops with olive oil and sprinkle with sea salt. Grill the bread until it's toasted and becomes crunchy. Grill the ramp tops just until they wilt. Note: If wild ramps are not available, baby leeks or scallions may be substituted.

HOW TO MAKE THE FAVA BEANS: Clean the fava beans by first shucking the beans from the husk. Set a large pot of water to boil. Blanch the beans in the skins for 3 minutes, then cool in ice water. Once cold, peel away the skins.

HOW TO PLATE: Remove the octopus from the dressing and mix with the grilled ramp tops, the pickled bottoms, and the fava beans. Serve with the grilled bread.

MAKES 24 TO 36 APPETIZER SERVINGS

Pacific Octopus with Preserved Lemon, Parsley Puree, and White Beans

For the Preserved Lemon
9 fresh lemons
1 teaspoon star anise, whole
1 teaspoon black pepper
1 teaspoon whole cloves
4 bay leaves
2 cups coarse sea salt
2 cinnamon sticks
1 cup olive oil

For the Parsley Puree
2 bunches Italian parsley
1 anchovy
1 garlic clove
1/4 cup extra-virgin olive oil
Fresh lemon juice, as needed
Pinch sea salt, to taste
1 16-ounce can navy (or white) beans

For the Octopus
4 seared jumbo octopus tentacles (tako)
Olive oil
Salt and pepper, to taste
2 preserved lemons

HOW TO MAKE THE PRESERVED LEMON: Making the preserved lemon takes about 1 week. If time is limited, preserved lemons may be purchased at most gourmet groceries. Juice 4 of the lemons. Wash the remaining lemons and cut into 4 sections, leaving the very end connected so they don't fall apart. Combine the star anise, black pepper, cloves, and bay leaves with the sea salt and stuff the lemons with as much spice filling as possible. Place the lemons in a sealed container with the fresh lemon juice and cinnamon sticks and refrigerate. Each day turn the lemons; on the 5th day add in the olive oil. On the 7th day, the lemons should be ready. Remove the pith (white part) from the lemons and discard the fruit. Slice the lemon skin as thin as possible. Any remaining whole lemon can be saved in the freezer for up to 6 months.

HOW TO MAKE THE PARSLEY PUREE: Wash the parsley and simply remove the bottom half of the stems. Save a few small tender leaves for garnish. In a large pot of boiling water, blanch the parsley for 3 minutes or until the stems are tender. Cool the cooked parsley in an icewater bath to stop the cooking process. Squeeze excess water from the parsley and blend with the anchovy, garlic, and half the olive oil until smooth. If the parsley won't puree easily, simply add a small amount of water.

HOW TO MAKE THE WHITE BEANS: If using canned beans, rinse the beans well to remove all the canning liquid before dressing the beans. Next, toss the beans with the parsley puree (reserving some for garnish). Adjust your seasoning with lemon juice, olive oil, and sea salt.

HOW TO MAKE THE OCTOPUS: Coat the tentacles with olive oil, and season with salt and pepper. Grill over high heat until slightly charred and warm. Slice the octopus into coins.

HOW TO PLATE: Divide the beans among individual serving plates. Top with the grilled octopus tentacles and garnish with the whole leaf parsley and sliced lemon rinds.

MAKES 4–6 SMALL APPETIZERS

"As the executive chef and owner of Farallon, Waterbar, and Nick's Cove in California, I decided long ago to keep a sustainable approach to what we have on our daily menu. A chef makes daily choices that are not solely to the presentation of a beautiful dish. Now more than ever our decisions affect the environment, and as consumers, the most valid action we can take is to choose wisely at the market."

—Executive Chef Mark Franz

Chapter 17

PACIFIC RAZOR CLAMS

EXECUTIVE CHEF MARK FRANZ—FARALLON

*T*he Pacific razor clam is a large species of clam found along the Pacific West Coast from the eastern Aleutian Islands, Alaska, to Pismo Beach, California. They inhabit sandy beaches in the intertidal zone down to a maximum depth of about 30 feet. This species has an elongated, oblong, narrow shell, which ranges from 3 to 6 inches in length in the southern portion of its range, with individuals up to 11 inches found in Alaska. It is similar to the smaller Atlantic razor clam, which is found on the East Coast of the United States.

Pacific razor clams are a highly desirable edible, collected both commercially and by recreational harvesters. Razor clams, like other shellfish, may sometimes accumulate dangerous levels of domoic acid, a marine toxin. Harvesters should be sure to check current public health recommendations before collecting razor clams. Razor clams are commonly battered and fried in butter, or made into a clam chowder.

Chef Mark Franz opened Farallon in June 1997, serving his sophisticated interpretation of "coastal cuisine." Chef Franz changes his menu daily, allowing him to highlight the freshest seafood available, as well as seasonal meat and game dishes. Farallon was nominated by the prestigious James Beard Foundation as one of the best restaurants in the country and was chosen as one of the best newcomers in the country by national magazines such as *Esquire, Bon Appetit,* and *Food and Wine.*

> "Pacific razor clams are one of my favorites because of the abundant succulent meat they have. Razor clams are glorious raw or fried, marinated or broiled."

With Lisa Weiss, Chef Franz wrote *The Farallon Cookbook* (Chronicle Books 2001). It highlights many of his signature dishes for which Farallon has become famous.

Broiled Razor Clams with Garlic Butter Bread Crumbs

½ cup fresh chopped bread crumbs

2 cloves garlic, peeled and finely chopped

3 ounces unsalted butter, melted

2 tablespoons fresh chopped Italian parsley

Pinch sea salt and pepper, to taste

4 fresh razor clams, shucked and chopped into ¼- or ½-inch pieces (clean and reserve shells)

How to make the razor clams: Mix the bread crumbs, garlic, melted butter, chopped parsley, sea salt, and pepper together in a bowl. Place equal amounts of clam meat into the four shells. Place the stuffed shells on a sheet pan and pack the buttered bread crumbs on the clam meat. Broil for 4 minutes.

Note: The trick is to have the broiler on for 10 minutes before you place the clams in the oven. Also, have the clams about 3 to 4 inches away from the heat source so they don't burn. Never take your eyes off the clams, as they may burn quickly. If necessary, lower the oven rack to slow the cooking process; just make sure not to overcook.

MAKES 2 SERVINGS (ALSO GREAT FOR PASSED APPETIZERS)

"When preparing live razor clams, use a sharp knife and cut off the black tip of the siphon. Next, open the body from the base of the foot to the tip of the siphon. Remove the gills, palps [mouth parts], and the stomach. Slit the digger so that it will lie flat. Pick out the small intestine that runs through the foot. Rinse in cold water and the razor clam steak is ready to use."

Orange and Rosemary Steamed Razor Clams with Fennel and Endive

HOW TO MAKE THE ORANGE AND ROSEMARY STEAMED RAZOR CLAMS: In a large pasta pot, pour in the cold water, the orange and lemon pulps, bay leaves, and half the rosemary, and bring to a boil. When water is boiling, place the clam meat in a colander and place above the boiling water. Cover with a lid and steam the clams over high heat for 4 minutes, stirring the clams halfway through the process to ensure they cook evenly. When finished steaming, add the cooked clam meat to a bowl and add half the orange and lemon juice, all the zest, the remaining rosemary, half the olive oil, and red chili flakes, and season with sea salt and pepper to taste. Toss well.

HOW TO MAKE THE FENNEL AND ENDIVE SALAD: Drain and spin-dry the fennel and Belgian endive. Add the remaining orange and lemon juice and extra-virgin olive oil, and season with sea salt and pepper. Toss to coat.

HOW TO PLATE: Arrange the endive and fennel in a ring at the edge of a serving platter and spoon the clams in the center. Pour the remaining liquid over the top and serve immediately.

MAKES 4 SERVINGS

2 quarts cold water
2 oranges, zest and juice both, pulp reserved
2 lemons, zest and juice both, pulp reserved
2 bay leaves
1 teaspoon finely chopped fresh rosemary
1 pound fresh razor clam meat, cut into ¼-inch slices
½ cup extra-virgin olive oil
1 teaspoon red chili flakes
Pinch sea salt and pepper, to taste
1 fresh fennel bulb, cored and sliced as thinly against the grain as possible (use a Japanese mandoline preferably) and soaked in lemon water to prevent discoloration
2 heads purple or white Belgian endive, cored and sliced ¼ inch thick lengthwise and soaked in lemon water to prevent discoloration

Pacific Razor Clam and Artichoke Crudo
with American Caviar and Yuzu

For the Crudo
4 baby artichokes, cleaned down to the yellow leaves (soak in lemon water to prevent discoloration)
12 ounces fresh razor clam meat, shucked, cleaned, and chopped
1 teaspoon fresh chives, sliced thinly on the bias
3 tablespoons grapeseed oil (or very light oil)
Pinch salt and pepper, to taste

For the Yuzu
1 ounce yuzu juice (or a blend of lemon and lime)
2½ ounces grapeseed oil
Pinch salt and pepper, to taste

For the Garnish
2 ounces American caviar (from the paddlefish; available at most gourmet groceries)
Toast points

How to make the clam crudo: Rinse, drain, and finely chop the artichokes and place into a glass bowl (no metal), along with the clams, chives, grapeseed oil, salt, and pepper, and mix well.

In another glass bowl, whisk the yuzu juice, grapeseed oil, salt, and pepper to combine.

How to plate: Spoon the clam mixture evenly into a 2-inch-wide ring mold in the center of each plate. Drizzle the yuzu sauce around the outside and top with the caviar. Garnish with the chives and toast points. Remove the ring mold before serving.

MAKES 4 SERVINGS

> "If you place live razor clams in the freezer for 30 minutes, you'll find they're easier to open."

"My first encounter with razor clams was in the fall of 1980. After having a good season guiding fly fishermen in the Brooks Range in Alaska, my boss flew a few of us out to the coast to dig razor clams. As we landed on the dark sandy beach, I could see we were far from alone. Below us were eight Alaskan brown bears up and down the beach, their heads in the sand digging clams! We spent the day avoiding the bears as we gathered lots of razor clams ourselves. That evening, we cleaned and cooked the clams in bacon fat and garlic right on the beach; believe it or not, the bears left us alone. A testament to how many clams they had eaten."

Linguine with Razor Clams, Anchovies, and Garlic

HOW TO MAKE THE LINGUINE WITH RAZOR CLAMS: Bring water to a boil; add salt. Cook the pasta in the boiling water until tender. This will take approximately 10 minutes (less if using fresh pasta). Meanwhile, heat the butter and oil in a saucepan. Stir in the garlic and anchovies. Simmer for 5 minutes. Add the clams and simmer 2 minutes. Add the parsley, capers, and egg yolks. Stir in the vinegar and mill in the black pepper. Allow contents to sit in the pan warm until the pasta is cooked.

HOW TO PLATE: Drain the pasta and add to the pan. Toss well and serve immediately.

MAKES 4 SERVINGS

4 quarts water
2 tablespoons salt
1 pound fresh linguine (or packaged)
4 tablespoons butter
2 tablespoons extra-virgin olive oil
1 clove garlic, minced
1 2-ounce can anchovy fillets
6 ounces fresh razor clams, chopped
4 tablespoons minced Italian parsley
1 teaspoon capers
4 hard-boiled egg yolks, chopped
2 tablespoons champagne vinegar
Liberal amount of fresh milled black pepper

> "If you are lucky enough to get live clams in the shell, soak them in cold salted water with a sprinkle of cornmeal overnight to purge out any sand."

Crispy Fried Razor Clams with Tamarind and Lime

For the Tamarind and Lime Sauce
2 tablespoons Thai fish sauce
1 tablespoon sugar
1 tablespoon tamarind paste
1 teaspoon fresh lime juice

For the Razor Clams
2 quarts peanut oil (or
  vegetable oil)
2 cups all-purpose flour
1 cup cornstarch
1 tablespoon salt
1 teaspoon pepper
1 pound fresh razor clam
  meat, cut into ¼-inch
  strips
12 fresh basil leaves
12 fresh cilantro leaves
12 fresh mint leaves

HOW TO MAKE THE TAMARIND AND LIME SAUCE: In a small saucepan, add the fish sauce, sugar, and tamarind paste, and bring to a boil. Allow to simmer for 2 minutes on medium-high heat until the sauce thickens slightly. Let cool and add the lime juice. Allow to sit at room temperature.

HOW TO MAKE THE FRIED RAZOR CLAMS: Heat the peanut oil in a pot that has at least 2 inches of room at the top so the oil will not bubble over when the clams are added. Heat to 375°F.

In a medium stainless steel bowl, mix the flour, cornstarch, salt, and pepper together. Toss the clam strips into the flour mixture and coat well. Use a wire-mesh strainer to shake the excess flour off the clams. Carefully add the clams to the hot oil, and fry for 1½ minutes, or until golden brown. Remove clams with a slotted spoon and drain on paper towel.

HOW TO PLATE: Place the hot fried clams in a bowl and toss with the fresh basil, cilantro, and mint leaves. Drizzle on the tamarind sauce until it lightly coats the clams. Serve immediately.

MAKES 4 SERVINGS

> "Razor clams cook very fast, so don't overcook them, as they get very tough if you do."

"Sustainable seafood is a must. Earth, though inappropriately named, is an ocean planet. We must protect our world's resources—the oceans—to sustain wildlife in the sea that we depend on day after day. We have come to learn all too quickly that the oceans cannot supply us endlessly if we do not take care of them. Sustainability takes management and making proper choices. We must take responsibility for our actions that affect our waters. Care and regulation hopefully will prevent future overfishing, habitat damage, pollution, and yes—global warming. That will give us the ability to sustain the fisheries population for our future generations."

—Executive Chef Allen Susser

Chapter 18

Pink Shrimp

Executive Chef Allen Susser—Chef Allen's Modern Seafood Grill

*J*udging from the enormous amount consumed each year, shrimp has become America's most popular shellfish. Among the hundreds of species that inhabit the world's seas is the northern pink shrimp, which dwells in Alaska's icy cold waters.

Commonly known as "bay shrimp," pink shrimp thrive on muddy ocean bottoms and prefer fairly deep water. Pink shrimp are trawl-caught using special nets. Large volumes of shrimp can be caught using this method; however, there is bycatch involved.

Pink shrimp have a sweet, delicate taste and are generally considered more flavorful than warm water varieties. Live, the tail of the pink shrimp is more red than pink. Cooked, the shell is pink and the meat is an opaque white tinged with pink. The meat is firm and crisp in texture, and moister than tropical shrimp.

Chef Allen Susser's pristine local fish and sustainable seafood make his Chef Allen's Modern Seafood Grill a must Miami destination.

Chef Susser is a prestigious James Beard Award winner and has many additional honors, including "Top Chef" by *Food and Wine Magazine*; Zagat Survey's "Best Restaurant for Food in Miami" (five years in a row); and *Gourmet Magazine*'s Top Table Award in South Florida. Chef Susser and his restaurant have been featured in the *Wall Street Journal, Time* magazine, *Bon Appetit, Food Arts,* and *Wine Spectator,* and he has appeared on NBC's *Today Show* as well as the CBS *Early Show*, WPBS, and the Food Network.

He is the original author of *New World Cuisine and Cookery, The Great Citrus Book,* and *The Great Mango Book.*

Pink Shrimp Waldorf Salad

HOW TO MAKE THE DRESSING: In a food processor, blend the vinegar, mustard, and oil. Blend in the cheese and the buttermilk. Transfer to a bowl and stir in the lemon zest, seasoning with salt and pepper.

HOW TO MAKE THE SHRIMP: In a large bowl, combine the pink shrimp with the mushrooms, walnuts, grapes, apples, celery, greens, and herbs. Toss with the dressing.

HOW TO PLATE: Arrange the salad on four plates. Spoon the shrimp and mushroom mixture over the top, and serve.

MAKES 4 SERVINGS

For the Dressing
1 tablespoon red wine vinegar
½ teaspoon dijon mustard
1 tablespoon olive oil
2 ounces blue cheese, crumbled
¼ cup buttermilk
½ teaspoon lemon zest
Pinch salt and pepper

For the Shrimp
1 pound Alaska pink shrimp, shelled, deveined, and cooked
1 cup enoki mushrooms
1 cup walnut halves, toasted
1 cup halved red seedless grapes
2 medium Fuji apples, cored and thinly sliced
2 ribs celery, thinly sliced
1 cup mesclun salad greens
2 tablespoons chopped parsley
2 tablespoons chopped tarragon
2 tablespoons snipped chives

> "Shrimp are one of the most seductive seafoods. Shrimp are one of my favorites, and I know I am not alone. After all, shrimp are the most popular seafood enjoyed by Americans. I guess you can say shrimp consumes us."

Pink Shrimp and Watermelon Salad

For the Shrimp

1 pound Alaska pink shrimp, shelled and deveined
1 teaspoon salt
2 large limes, juiced
2 teaspoons soy sauce
1 teaspoon sugar
3 tablespoons cold water
1 tablespoon sesame oil

For the Salad

1 tablespoon pickled jalapeños
2 cups 1-inch-cubed watermelon
1 cup colorful cherry tomatoes
1 bunch frisee, cleaned to yellow centers
2 tablespoons freshly chopped tarragon
1 small orange, juiced
1 small lemon, juiced
1/4 cup extra-virgin olive oil
1 teaspoon kosher salt
1 teaspoon coarse black pepper
1 teaspoon black sesame seeds

HOW TO MAKE THE SHRIMP: In a small stainless steel bowl, mix the shrimp with the salt, lime juice, soy, sugar, and cold water. Let marinate for half an hour. Strain and dry with paper towels before cooking. Place on a dry plate.

In a heavy wok pan over high heat, drizzle in the sesame oil. Stir in the shrimp and wok sauté for 2 to 3 minutes until the shrimp turn golden brown.

HOW TO MAKE THE SALAD: Combine the jalapeños, watermelon, tomatoes, and frisee. Toss with a vinaigrette made by whisking together the tarragon, orange juice, lemon juice, olive oil, salt, and pepper.

HOW TO PLATE: Arrange the watermelon salad on a platter. Place the sizzle and spice shrimp in the center. Finish the salad with black sesame seeds.

MAKES 6 SERVINGS

"The best way to keep shrimp fresh is to keep them very chilled while not directly exposed to ice or water. When storing shrimp in a refrigerator, keep them in a tightly sealed ziplock bag with another ziplock filled with ice on top."

Pink Shrimp with Vanilla Mojo

3 tablespoons olive oil
1 large onion, cut into 1/4-inch dice
2 cloves garlic, minced
1 tablespoon ground cumin
1 teaspoon dried oregano
1 tablespoon kosher salt
1 teaspoon freshly ground black pepper
1 piece vanilla bean, split open
1 cup freshly squeezed orange juice
1 tablespoon light rum
1/4 cup freshly squeezed lime juice
1 large plantain, cut in small coins
16 Alaska pink shrimp, peeled and cleaned

HOW TO MAKE THE SHRIMP MOJO: In a medium saucepan over medium heat, heat olive oil. Add the onion, garlic, cumin, oregano, salt, pepper, and vanilla bean, cooking for 3 to 4 minutes. Pour in the orange juice, rum, lime juice, and plantains. Bring the mixture to a simmer, cooking for 15 minutes until the plantain is tender. Stir in the shrimp and let the mojo return to a boil. Turn off the heat, and cover the shrimp mojo. Allow to rest for 3 minutes before serving.

MAKES 4 SERVINGS

"Shrimp prefer deep water by day and fairly shallow water by night. I discovered this years back when I moved to Miami from New York City. One late night, I was headed across the causeway that runs very close to Biscayne Bay's water's edge on my way home from Miami Beach. All of a sudden, down off the road, I saw flashes of light seemingly coming out of the water. I couldn't imagine what was going on. So I pulled over to explore. Not one or two, but now there were a dozen or so swaying lights. I saw these lights were flashlights being pointed into the shallow water. There I spied eight or nine guys in small groups shouting to each other. They were throwing nets from the shoreline and from small skiffs. This was a spectacle in the shadows of the Miami neon-lit skyline. They were shrimping! I loved it. Right here in my backyard these guys were pulling live flapping and flittering shrimp from the water. I found out these old Cuban guys come out every full moon to pull shrimp. I thought to join them, but on second thought I pulled out $20 and bought a big bucket of their live shrimp catch. Off I raced to my kitchen to cook my shrimp catch while they were still kicking."

Pink Shrimp and Organic Grits

HOW TO MAKE THE GRITS: Using a medium-size saucepan, bring the milk to a boil and lower to a simmer. Add the grits while whisking, continuing to whisk for 5 minutes until smooth. Stir every 5 minutes for an additional 30 to 40 minutes. If the grits get too thick too quickly, add more milk. Check for doneness when grits hold shape when spooned, still al dente but creamy. Whisk in the butter and cheese, and season with salt.

HOW TO MAKE THE SHRIMP: Warm a large, heavy skillet over high heat. Drizzle with olive oil, adding the shallots and chorizo. Quickly sauté and add the shrimp, cooking until pink. Add the tamarind syrup and orange juice, and season with the remaining salt and the pepper.

HOW TO PLATE: Give the grits a final stir, adding the scallions. Pour into a large bowl. Spoon the shrimp over the grits and serve.

MAKES 8 TO 10 SERVINGS

3 cups whole milk
1 cup organic grits
2 tablespoons unsalted butter
2 tablespoons manchego cheese, grated
$\frac{1}{2}$ teaspoon kosher salt
2 tablespoons olive oil
2 tablespoons minced shallots
1 tablespoon smoked chorizo
18 Alaska pink shrimp, peeled and cleaned
1 tablespoon tamarind syrup
3 tablespoons fresh orange juice
$\frac{1}{2}$ teaspoon freshly ground black pepper
1 teaspoon chopped scallions

"Shrimp is a fast-selling item, so it is often displayed alongside other, slower-moving seafood. Remember that pink shrimp are cooked and ready to eat, so do not let them come into contact with raw seafood, or bacterial contamination may result."

Pink Shrimp with Green Chilis and Lime

2 tablespoons fresh
   squeezed lime juice
1 tablespoon Thai fish sauce
   (found in Asian markets)
1 tablespoon sugar
1 stalk fresh lemongrass
1 tablespoon thickly sliced
   (ovals) fresh green serrano
   chili
1 large shallot, thinly sliced
½ pound Alaska pink shrimp,
   peeled and deveined with
   tails left on
½ cup chicken stock or
   water
1 handful fresh mint leaves
3 leaves Boston lettuce or
   other leaf lettuce

HOW TO MAKE THE MARINADE: Combine the lime juice, fish sauce, and sugar in a small bowl. Stir well, dissolving the sugar completely. Taste and adjust the flavor to your liking. Set aside. Trim the lemongrass to a smooth, clean, 3-inch stalk, measured from the root end of the bulb. Discard any rough root ends, tops, and dry, tough outer leaves. Slice the trimmed stalk crosswise into paper-thin circles, which should reveal purple-edged swirls. Add to the marinade with the chilis and shallots.

HOW TO MAKE THE SHRIMP: Combine the shrimp and chicken stock in a small skillet. Cook gently over low heat until the shrimp turn pink and are opaque and firm, 1 to 2 minutes. Turn them once, just before they're done. Remove the pan from the heat as the stock starts to boil, and scoop the shrimp out with a slotted spoon into a medium bowl. Add the lime juice mixture, chilis, shallot, and lemongrass to the bowl with the shrimp. Using your hands, mix well. Break up chunks of shallot and lemongrass into smaller sections. Stir in most of the mint leaves, reserving a few leaves for garnish.

HOW TO PLATE: Arrange the lettuce leaves on a small serving platter. With a slotted spoon, transfer the shrimp mixture to the platter, mounding it on the lettuce. Spoon some of the sauce over the shrimp and garnish with the remaining mint. Serve immediately.

MAKES 4 SERVINGS

"Sustainable seafood will help ensure that my kids and grandkids will be also able to enjoy the treasures of the sea like king crab."

—Executive Chef John Ash

Chapter 19

RED KING CRAB

EXECUTIVE CHEF JOHN ASH—JOHN ASH AND COMPANY

The king crab is the largest crab in U.S. waters. They are characterized by their massive size, long, spidery legs, and spiny exteriors. There are three common species of king crab—red king crab, blue king crab, and brown (golden) king crab. Red king crab is the most sought after. The meat is the sweetest, and the legs are always packed full.

Most of the king crab on the U.S. market is currently supplied by Russian Far East fisheries, where management is very poor and stocks are severely overfished. Therefore, imported king crab should be avoided. King crab from Alaska is the better choice where the Alaskan king crab fishery is well managed and fishing grounds are closed in many areas to allow stocks to recover.

Chef John Ash, also known as the "Father of Wine Country Cuisine," opened his namesake restaurant, John Ash and Company, in Santa Rosa, California, in 1980. It was the first restaurant in the Northern California wine country to focus on local, seasonal ingredients to create dishes that complemented the wines being made in the region. It continues to be critically acclaimed today.

Chef Ash has moved on to many other ventures since that first restaurant, including writing award-winning cookbooks, co-hosting *The Good Food Hour*, a radio talk show, hosting his own TV show on the Food Network, and teaching cooking classes. He is an adjunct instructor at the Culinary Institute of America at Greystone in the Napa Valley, and in 2008 he was voted "Cooking School Teacher of the Year" by the International Association of Culinary Professionals. His passion for teaching is matched only by his passionate voice on sustainable food issues, serving on the board of the Chef's Collaborative, a national organization committed to sustainable and ethical food issues, and the Board of Advisors of Seafood Watch.

Red King Crab in Wine and Vermouth

2 pounds cooked king crab
  legs
¼ pound unsalted butter
⅔ cup vermouth
½ cup dry white wine
1½ cups chicken stock
3 tablespoons thinly sliced
  garlic
2 teaspoons minced fresh
  ginger
1½ tablespoons soy sauce
1 tablespoon fresh lemon
  juice
2 teaspoons sugar
2 teaspoons cornstarch,
  dissolved in 1 tablespoon
  water
¼ cup chopped fresh parsley
  (or a combination of
  parsley and chives)
Freshly ground black pepper,
  to taste

HOW TO MAKE THE RED KING CRAB IN WINE AND VERMOUTH:
Crack and separate the crab into sections and set aside.

Place the butter, vermouth, white wine, chicken stock, garlic, ginger, soy sauce, lemon juice, sugar, and cornstarch in a saucepan and simmer, covered, for 5 minutes or so. Add the crab, parsley, and pepper, and warm crab through.

HOW TO PLATE: Divide into large bowls with the broth and serve immediately.

MAKES 2 SERVINGS (OR 4 AS AN APPETIZER)

"Many years ago, I had the opportunity to board a crab boat in Alaska. At the time I had never seen a live king crab and had no idea how large and menacing they could be. As a hands-on observer, I tried to help unload a trap, but after getting pinched several times—drawing blood—I backed off. I can truly appreciate how difficult and dangerous king crab fishing is, particularly in the Bering Sea."

SHELLFISH, MOLLUSKS, AND OTHERS

Red King Crab Newburg

For the Crab Butter (makes about ¼ cup)
Shells from 1 pound king crab
½ cup (1 stick) unsalted butter

For the Crab Newburg
¼ cup (½ stick) crab butter
1 pound cooked king crab meat, picked over to remove bits of shell
2 tablespoons plus 1 teaspoon medium-dry sherry, such as amontillado
3 tablespoons plus 1 teaspoon brandy
1½ cups heavy cream
¼ teaspoon freshly grated nutmeg
Cayenne and salt, to taste
4 large egg yolks, beaten well in a medium bowl
Drops of lemon juice
Brioche toast points
1 tablespoon fresh chopped chives

HOW TO MAKE THE CRAB BUTTER: Spread 1 pound of dry shells from king crab legs on a baking sheet and toast them in a preheated 325°F oven for 15 to 20 minutes. Break the shells as finely as you can using a mallet, mortar and pestle, or rolling pin. Melt the butter in a double boiler over gently simmering water, add the shells, and cook for 10 minutes. Set aside for 15 to 20 minutes to let flavors infuse. Pour into a fine-mesh strainer set over a bowl and press gently but firmly with a rubber spatula to strain out all the butter. Refrigerate, and discard any liquid after the butter has solidified.

HOW TO MAKE THE RED KING CRAB NEWBURG: In a heavy saucepan, heat the butter over medium heat. Add the crab, 2 tablespoons of the sherry, and 2 tablespoons of brandy, and cook, stirring for 2 minutes, or until heated through.

Transfer the crabmeat with a slotted spoon to a bowl. Add the cream to the sherry mixture remaining in the pan and boil until it is reduced to about 1 cup. Reduce the heat to low and stir in the remaining 1 teaspoon sherry, the nutmeg, the cayenne, and salt, to taste. Slowly whisk the cream mixture into the yolks and return to the stove over moderate heat. Stirring constantly, cook the mixture until it thickens nicely, another minute or so, being careful not to scramble the eggs. Stir in the crabmeat and finish with drops of lemon juice, to taste.

HOW TO PLATE: Serve the crab mixture over toast points and top with the chopped chives.

MAKES 4 SERVINGS

Tomatillo, Corn, and King Crab Chowder

Note: Fresh poblano chilis are widely available and often incorrectly labeled *pasilla* in many supermarkets.

HOW TO MAKE THE CHOWDER: In a soup pot, add the oil and over moderate heat cook the onions, garlic, and chilis until just beginning to color, about 6 minutes. Add the stock and tomatillos and simmer for 5 minutes or so, until vegetables are just tender. Add the crab and corn and simmer until heated through, about 3 minutes. You can add a bit more stock if desired. Add the tomatoes and season to your taste with salt and pepper.

To get even more corn flavor, simmer the corncobs in the stock for a few minutes. Discard them before adding stock to recipe.

HOW TO PLATE: Divide the avocado and cilantro among four bowls. Ladle the hot chowder over and serve immediately.

MAKES 4 SERVINGS

2 tablespoons olive oil
2 cups sliced onion
1 tablespoon thinly slivered garlic
1 large poblano chili, stemmed, seeded, and cut into large dice
2 teaspoons seeded and chopped serrano chili (optional)
5 cups (or so) low-salt, defatted chicken stock
2 cups tomatillos, husked, rinsed, and cut in half or quarters if too large
1 pound cooked king crabmeat, picked over to remove bits of shell
1½ cups fresh or frozen corn kernels
1 cup fresh or canned diced tomatoes
Pinch salt and freshly ground pepper, to taste
1 medium avocado, peeled, pitted, and coarsely chopped
¼ cup coarsely chopped fresh cilantro

"Because king crab has such a meaty presence in whatever recipe you use king crab, it is most important to serve it as simple as possible. Don't complicate or even ruin the dish with sauces and seasonings. Allow the purity of the crab to come through."

Red King Crab with Avocado, Roasted Beets, Crème Fraiche, and Lime

For the Roasted Beets
12 small golden beets
2 tablespoons extra-virgin
 olive oil, divided
Kosher salt and pepper, to
 taste
Juice ½ lemon

For the Jalapeño Lime Vinaigrette
¼ cup finely diced shallots
2 teaspoons seeded and
 diced jalapeños
2 tablespoons wildflower
 honey
⅓ cup fresh lime juice
Pinch kosher salt and pepper,
 to taste
½ cup olive oil

For the King Crab
2 medium, firm, ripe Hass
 avocados
Pinch kosher salt and pepper,
 to taste
1 bunch fresh watercress,
 cleaned, with tough stems
 removed
¾ pound cooked king
 crabmeat, picked over to
 remove bits of shell
1 tablespoon fresh chopped
 parsley
1 tablespoon fresh chopped
 cilantro
½ cup crème fraiche

HOW TO MAKE THE BEETS: Preheat the oven to 400°F. Cut the leaves and stems from the beets. Clean the beets well, toss them with 1 tablespoon of olive oil, and season with salt and pepper. Place the beets in a roasting pan with a splash of water in the bottom. Cover with foil and roast 30 to 40 minutes, until tender when pierced with a toothpick. When the beets are done, carefully remove the foil. Let cool and peel the beets by rubbing with a paper towel. Cut the beets into ½-inch wedges. Toss them in a medium bowl with 1 tablespoon or so of olive oil, a generous squeeze of lemon juice, and a sprinkling of salt and pepper. Taste for seasoning.

HOW TO MAKE THE JALAPEÑO LIME VINAIGRETTE: Combine the shallots, jalapeños, honey, lime juice, and salt and pepper in a small bowl and let it sit for 5 minutes. Whisk in about ½ cup olive oil and taste for balance and seasoning.

HOW TO PLATE: Cut the avocados in half lengthwise, remove the pit and peel. Cut into ⅓-inch slices and season with salt and pepper. Fan the avocado slices on one side of a chilled platter. Place the beets on the other side and arrange the watercress in the center. Toss the crab gently with ⅔ of the jalapeño lime vinaigrette, the parsley, and the cilantro in a large bowl. Taste the crab and season with more salt or lime if you like. Pile the crab on the watercress and top with the crème fraiche.

MAKES 4 SERVINGS

"King crab legs are always previously fro-
zen with a layer of ice, which protects them during trans-
portation. Though you can defrost them in cold water,
it's best to defrost king crab legs slowly in the refrigerator by submerging them in water. This will allow the legs
to retain their wonderfully briny flavor."

Red King Crab with Mango and Celery Root and Apple Salad

HOW TO MAKE THE CELERY ROOT AND APPLE SALAD: Peel the celery root, thinly slice into rounds, and cut the root into thin julienne. In a separate bowl, mix together the mayonnaise, buttermilk, mustards, and lemon juice until smooth. Season to taste with the salt, pepper, and paprika. Set ¼ cup or so aside to mix with the crab. Next, gently stir the celery root and apple into the remaining mayonnaise mixture to evenly coat. This is best done at least an hour ahead and chilled for the flavors to develop.

Note: Celery root can vary widely. Pick ones that are heavy for their size, which means there won't be a hole in the center. Taste the celery root after cutting, and if it seems tough or too strongly flavored, then blanch it for a few seconds in salted boiling water followed by a dunk in ice water to retain its crunch. The celery root salad can be made a day or two ahead and stored covered and refrigerated. If you want greens in this salad, the addition of some young, white frisée and/or cress tossed with a little olive oil and lemon would be nice banked around the salad.

HOW TO PLATE: Using a 3-inch round mold, mound the celery root in the center on plates. Top with the mango and then crab mixed with the reserved dressing from the celery root salad. Press down gently to form a relatively compact cake. Remove ring mold and repeat with remaining plates, dividing the ingredients equally. Top each with caviar and chervil sprigs and serve immediately.

MAKES 8 SERVINGS, AS A STARTER COURSE

1 small celery root (½ pound)
⅔ cup mayonnaise
2 tablespooons buttermilk
1½ tablespoons whole grain mustard
1½ tablespoons smooth dijon mustard
2 teaspoons fresh lemon juice
Pinch salt and freshly ground pepper, to taste
Large pinch hot paprika or cayenne
1 small Fuji or other tart-sweet apple, peeled, cored, and julienned
1 large ripe mango, peeled and diced
1 pound king crab, picked over to remove bits of shell
2 ounces fresh salmon or trout caviar*
Chervil sprigs, for garnish

*Two favorite sources for salmon and trout caviars are Tsar Nicoulai in California and Sunburst Trout Farms in North Carolina.

> "Alaskan king crab has loads of deliciously sweet meat relative to the shell, making king crab a better bargain than the price may indicate. King crab is also extremely versatile."

"Before you buy your seafood, ask questions. Find out which seafood you should purchase as a wild-caught variety and which should be farm-raised. For the ethically minded, learn the difference between seafood harvested in U.S. waters and those brought in from overseas. All these elements play a vital role in purchasing the best and freshest seafood available."

—Executive Chef Kaz Sato

Chapter 20

RED SEA URCHIN

EXECUTIVE CHEF KAZ SATO—KAI SUSHI

*R*ed sea urchins are harvested for their roe, called "uni," which is considered an aphrodisiac by some. Inside the sea urchin are five yellowish-orange strips arranged in a star-shaped pattern. These strips are the roe or uni. Uni has a very sweet flavor and delicate texture. It is generally consumed chilled. High-quality uni is mainly sold on auction at the major wholesale markets. Factors affecting the price include freshness, color, shape, firmness, and taste. Uni is a delicacy in Japan and at sushi bars worldwide.

The red sea urchin is commercially harvested by hand by local divers. Harvesting takes place at depths of 5 to 100 feet. Sea urchins are collected from the ocean bottom with a handheld rake or hook and put into a hoop net bag or wire basket.

Born in Tokyo, Japan, Chef Kaz Sato, owner and executive chef of Kai Sushi in Santa Barbara, California, received his culinary credentials at Shinjuku Culinary School before working at notable establishments in Jogashima—Japan's premiere fishing area and fish market on the Miura-hanto Peninsula. Chef Sato elevated his career when he became a chef at the prestigious Tokyo Kaikan. When he accepted Tokyo Kaikan's invitation to open a restaurant in Los Angeles, he relocated to the United States, and, after a stint as head chef for Sushi Zen in Oregon, he opened Kai Sushi. More than twenty-five years later, Chef Sato continues to serve up traditional Japanese cuisine infused with his unique artistic flare.

Chef Sato is also the co-author of *The Idiot's Guide to Sushi and Sashimi*, proving that making delicious sushi and sashimi in the comfort and convenience of your own home is not a daunting task. ✌

I'll Have Another

Kai Sushi sits on the bustling corner of De La Guerra and State Streets in Santa Barbara, California. It is here, at this popular eatery, that fresh uni is delivered daily.

Inside, at the sushi bar, where a wonderfully controlled chaos abounds, head chef Kaz Sato is chatting with a visitor from Boston.

"Yes, ma'am," he replies politely to the inquiring woman, who points to an unfamiliar seafood behind the glass, "that is uni, fresh sea urchin roe from Santa Barbara waters. Very good!"

"How do you eat it?" the woman asks inquisitively, staring at the soft, yellow-orange custard-like substance as if not quite sold on the idea.

"You can sauté it, add it to a bowl of pasta, but I recommend eating it fresh from the sea."

"And it's good?"

"Very, very good!"

Kaz prepares an oval clump of sushi rice topped with a strip of bright-yellow sea urchin roe, and offers it to her—on the house.

She smiles . . . hesitates . . . and takes a bite.

"Interesting," she says. "And delicious."

"Fishermen call uni the 'caviar of the sea,'" Kaz says with his signature smile. "The roe is firm, rich, and has a dense floral taste with the aroma of rose petals."

"Then perhaps I'll have another," the woman replies.

Fresh Sea Urchin Roe with Lemon and Lime

To make the sea urchin: Using a sharp pair of kitchen scissors, carefully remove the top of the live urchin as you would a pumpkin, avoiding the sharp spines and being careful not to damage the delicate roe inside. It may be necessary to use a heavy knife to crack the top before inserting the scissors. Inside the urchin are five yellow strips, resembling "little tongues," that run from top to bottom. This is the urchin roe or uni. Carefully run a small utensil like a butter knife under the roe along the inside of the shell to loosen. The roe is incredibly fragile, so try not to break the pieces. The secret to eating urchin is to understand how delicate the roe is. Remove the intact pieces of roe and place in a chilled plastic dish (as heat will dissolve the roe). Using fingers or tweezers, clean each piece of roe by removing any particles, such as partly digested seaweed or viscera. When the roe is clean, give it a quick rinse in fresh water. The roe should be well drained, especially if they are not to be eaten immediately.

How to plate: With the roe removed, carefully hollow out the urchin shell, like you would a pumpkin, being cautious not to break the spines. Fill the shell with shaved ice. Place the strips of roe in a star-shaped pattern on the ice. Cover with the urchin top and place on a serving platter, accompanied by an assortment of crackers and wedges of lemon and lime.

MAKES 2–4 SERVINGS

1–2 live red sea urchin
Shaved ice
Cracker assortment
Lemon wedges
Lime wedges

Red Sea Urchin "Uni" Shooter

½ ounce ponzu sauce (to make, mix equal parts of lemon juice, rice vinegar, sake, water, and a pinch of minced dry seaweed)

2–3 pieces fresh sea urchin roe (uni)

1 quail egg (yolk only)

Pinch finely sliced scallion (damp dry with paper towel)

Pinch chili daikon (to make, mix a fine-quality store-bought chili sauce with finely shredded white radish)

TO MAKE THE SHOOTER: Fill a shot glass half full with ponzu sauce. Add 2 or 3 pieces of fresh uni, depending on the size of the glass. Carefully add the yolk of egg, careful not to break. Top off with a pinch of sliced scallion and chili daikon. Bottoms up!

MAKES 1 SERVING

SHELLFISH, MOLLUSKS, AND OTHERS

Chapter 21

SNOW CRAB

EXECUTIVE CHEF ROB KINNEEN—ORSO

*T*he snow crab, also called opilio or tanner crab, is smaller than king crab with a leg span usually less than 2 feet and a total weight of 1 to 2 pounds. Snow crabs are captured using large metal-framed traps, called pots. Harvesting of females is prohibited by law, and only the males of the commercially acceptable and legal minimum size are harvested.

Together, the United States (Alaska) and Canada account for the majority of the snow crab on the U.S. market. Denmark (Greenland) and Russia supply the rest. Such "imported" crab should be avoided, as Far East fisheries are not as clearly regulated—or regulations are not as strictly enforced—as those in the North American markets.

Chef Robert Kinneen, executive chef at Orso, spends his days looking for, cooking with, and promoting the best Alaska has to offer and refining the concept of Alaskan regional cuisine.

Chef Kinneen attended the Culinary Institute of America in Hyde Park, New York, and after graduation he fine-tuned his skills in all facets of the industry while working at several prestigious restaurants that include NOLA in New Orleans, Sack's Cafe in Anchorage, and The Magnolia Grill, Pop's Trattoria, and Elaine's on Franklin in North Carolina. During this time he established his philosophies of sourcing products locally and seasonally. Returning to Alaska in 2001, he maintained the AAA four-diamond rating as chef of the Seven Glaciers restaurant at the Alyeska Resort and chef de cuisine at the Crow's Nest atop the Hotel Captain Cook. He is currently executive chef at Orso, a Mediterranean restaurant with an emphasis on Alaskan ingredients and a commitment to building relationships with Alaskan fishermen, farmers, and producers.

"I really enjoy the immense flavor of snow crab. The crab has a nice, tender texture and subtle sweetness which is very delicious."

Alaska Snow Crab Fritter with Alder-Smoked Mustard Aioli

HOW TO MAKE THE SNOW CRAB FRITTERS: In a large bowl, combine the flour, egg, milk, cayenne, salt, and pepper. Fold in the onion, celery, garlic, and crabmeat.

Fill a heavy-bottomed 3-quart pot about 3 inches deep with safflower or peanut oil. Heat to 325°F. Carefully add the fritters (1-ounce scoop portions) and cook for 3 to 4 minutes, flipping occasionally. Remove from the oil and drain on paper towels.

HOW TO MAKE THE AIOLI: In a medium bowl, add the yolks, mustard, garlic, and salt. Whisk until well incorporated. Add the vinegar and continue to whisk (about 30 seconds). Add a steady stream of the olive oil, pausing to make sure the mixture incorporates. When the ingredients have emulsified, add the Alaskan mustard and mix thoroughly.

HOW TO PLATE: Arrange the crab fritters on a large serving platter and place the aioli in the center.

MAKES 5 SERVINGS

For the Fritters
3/4 cup all-purpose flour
1 egg
1/2 cup milk
Pinch cayenne pepper
Pinch salt
Pinch pepper
1/2 yellow onion, diced small
1 stalk celery, diced small
1 garlic clove, smashed
1 cup shelled Alaska snow crab
Safflower or peanut oil

For the Alder-Smoked Mustard Aioli
2 egg yolks
1/2 teaspoon dijon mustard
1 clove garlic, minced
Pinch kosher salt
3 tablespoons cider vinegar
6 ounces olive oil
3 tablespoons alder-smoked Alaskan mustard (or high-quality whole grain mustard)

"I was born and raised in Petersburg, Alaska, where most of my experience with crab originated. I remember one day my mother trying to boil some snow crab for a family get-together. Let's just say the crab were not excited about the situation. As I heard my mom scream, I saw and heard a tic-tic-tic as some of the crab got loose and scuttled across the floor for a great escape. It was not to be. I gathered the loose crab, gave my mom a hand, and dinner was served on time to family and friends."

Pan-Seared Alaska Snow Crab–Stuffed Risotto Cakes with Winter Salad

For the Snow Crab Stock (makes 2 quarts)
2 tablespoons olive oil
4 cloves garlic, smashed
1 onion, roughly chopped
5 pounds Alaska snow crab shells, cracked
2 cups white wine
2½ quarts water

For the Risotto Cakes
Olive oil, as needed
2 ounces small-diced yellow onion
2 ounces small-diced celery
1 clove garlic, minced
1 cup Arborio rice
½ cup white wine
3 cups fresh crab stock
¼ ounce salt
¼ ounce pepper
8 ounces shelled Alaska snow crab, excess moisture squeezed out (particularly from the body)
3 ounces semolina flour

For the Winter Salad
1 small fennel bulb, shaved thin
2 apples (preferably Granny Smith), julienned with skin on
½ celery root, outer skin removed, thinly julienned
Juice 1 lemon
2 tablespoons chopped fresh parsley
1 tablespoon birch syrup (available online)
2 ounces olive oil
Pinch salt and pepper, to taste

HOW TO MAKE THE SNOW CRAB STOCK: In a heavy-bottomed stockpot over medium heat, add the olive oil and sweat the garlic and onion. Add the crab shells and white wine, and reduce the wine by half. Add the water, bring to a boil, then to a simmer. Continue to cook for 20 to 25 minutes, skimming frequently. Strain through a colander and then through a fine-mesh sieve. The stock is now ready to use.

HOW TO MAKE THE RISOTTO CAKES: In a stockpot over medium, heat 2 ounces of olive oil. Add the onion, celery, and garlic, and sauté for several minutes. Add the rice and another ounce or two of oil to coat the rice. Stir well. Add the wine, stirring frequently. Add the snow crab stock, 1 cup at a time, stirring frequently. When all the liquid is incorporated, and the risotto is firm to the bite but cooked through, remove from heat and spread out the rice on a sheet pan. Allow to cool.

Divide the rice into 2-ounce portions and roll into balls. With your thumb, make a divot in the center and stuff with the snow crab meat (about 1 ounce). Refashion into a ball, and then flatten into a cake that's thin enough to pan-fry. Dust each cake with semolina flour. Cook in a large sauté pan over medium heat with about ½ inch of oil. Cook the cakes for 1 minute per side, making sure they don't get too dark. Season with salt and pepper.

HOW TO MAKE THE WINTER SALAD: Toss the shaved fennel bulb and julienned apple and celery root. Add the lemon juice and parsley, and drizzle the birch syrup and olive oil. Season with salt and pepper.

HOW TO PLATE: Place the cakes on a serving platter or individual appetizer plates, and top with the winter salad.

MAKES 4 SERVINGS

SHELLFISH, MOLLUSKS, AND OTHERS

Zucchini Timbale Stuffed with Alaska Snow Crab Salad and Marinated Carrot Tangle

4 zucchini (12–14 inches long), sliced thin lengthwise (approximately 14–16 slices per zucchini)
2 fresh carrots, peeled into long strips down to the core
3 ounces olive oil, divided
2 ounces small-diced onion
2 ounces small-diced celery
2 ounces small-diced red pepper
2 cloves garlic, minced
3 ounces mayonnaise
12 ounces shelled Alaska snow crab
1 tablespoon fresh chopped parsley
1 tablespoon fresh chopped tarragon
1 tablespoon finely cut fresh chives
Salt and pepper, to taste

HOW TO MAKE THE STUFFED ZUCCHINI TIMBALE: Bring a pot of salted water to a boil. Blanch the zucchini for 30 to 40 seconds and quickly remove. Place the zucchini in an icewater bath for about 1 minute to stop the cooking process. Remove and let cool. Repeat the process with the carrots. In a sauté pan over medium heat, add the olive oil and sweat the onion, celery, red pepper, and garlic. When the onions are translucent, add to a bowl and let cool. Add the mayonnaise and crabmeat and toss well to combine.

HOW TO PLATE: Using 4 smooth-edged tea or coffee cups (6 ounces) or the like, place the zucchini in a circular pattern to cover the interior circumference of each mold. Add the crab salad to each cup, making sure there is enough room for the zucchini ends to fold over the top of the cup. Close the zucchini to encase the mold and flip onto a plate. Toss the blanched carrots with the parsley, tarragon, chives, and olive oil, and season with salt and pepper. Place on top of the zucchini and serve.

MAKES 4 SERVINGS

"The most important point to remember when acquiring crab—or any seafood—is to use the seafood within a respectable amount of time."

Chilled English Pea Soup with Alaska Snow Crab and Roasted Chanterelles

HOW TO MAKE THE PEA SOUP: In a medium-size pot over medium heat, add 1 tablespoon olive oil and sweat the shallots, making sure not to brown. Deglaze with the white wine and reduce by half. Add the vegetable or crab broth and bring to a boil. When the liquid returns to a boil, add the peas. Turn off the heat and let steep for 1 minute. Using a blender, puree the soup and allow to chill. Season with salt and pepper (note: when you serve items chilled, the flavoring will not be as enhanced). Next, roll the mushrooms in ½ tablespoon olive oil, salt, and pepper, place on a baking sheet, and bake in the oven at 350°F. Roast for 8 to 10 minutes, or until the mushrooms are cooked through.

HOW TO PLATE: Divide the soup among individual soup bowls and garnish with the mushrooms and crab on top.

MAKES 4 SERVINGS

1½ tablespoons olive oil, divided
4 ounces sliced shallots
1 cup dry white wine
12 ounces vegetable or crab broth
12 ounces fresh English (sweet) peas
Pinch kosher salt and white pepper, to taste
8 ounces chanterelle mushrooms, torn into quarters
Pinch salt and pepper
4 ounces shelled Alaska snow crab meat

"Never throw away crab shells. I always like to use the shells to make a quick stock. . . . There is a tremendous amount of flavor when using crab shells, and crafting a homemade stock is relatively easy."

Alaska Snow Crab Oscar Bites with Bearnaise Aioli

For the Bites
6 ounces beef tenderloin, cut into 8 3/4-ounce 1-inch cubes

Pinch salt and pepper, to taste

6 ounces shelled Alaska snow crab

For the Bearnaise Aioli
2 egg yolks

1 clove garlic, minced

1/2 teaspoon dijon mustard

Pinch kosher salt

3 tablespoons cider vinegar

6 ounces pomace olive oil

For the Reduction
4 ounces champagne vinegar

1 ounce shallots, minced

1/2 ounce fresh tarragon (reserve half for garnish, chop the rest)

Translucent toothpicks

1/4 pound fresh asparagus, blanched and cut on bias

HOW TO MAKE THE SNOW CRAB OSCAR BITES: Season the cubed beef with salt and pepper and sear on each side over medium heat, to your preferred doneness (medium-rare suggested). Cool the beef and reserve. For best appearance, use the upper leg portions of the snow crab. Be sure to clean the thin cartilage out of the leg meat.

HOW TO MAKE THE BEARNAISE AIOLI: Combine the egg yolks, garlic, mustard, salt, vinegar, and olive oil in a bowl and mix well.

HOW TO MAKE THE REDUCTION: For the reduction, add the champagne vinegar to a saucepan over medium heat. Add the shallots, and sauté while reducing the vinegar by three-quarters. Remove from heat, cool, and fold in the aioli. Add the tarragon to the reduction-aioli mixture and fold in to combine.

HOW TO PLATE: On each toothpick, alternate asparagus, crab, and beef. Dollop each with 1/2 ounce of bearnaise aioli, and plate. Garnish with tarragon.

MAKES 4 SERVINGS

"All of our seafood at Orso is wild, and Alaskan whenever possible. We have partnerships with many Alaskan seafood providers, which work closely with the fishermen and have set up stringent restrictions as to how the seafood is handled. We Alaskans are proud of our sustainable infrastructure in order to preserve our natural bounty."

—Executive Chef Rob Kinneen

"As a chef, I feel obliged to think about sustainability. I am responsible for serving a great deal of seafood and I must think about the future. I strive to work as close to the product as possible, and we do our best to only serve sustainable seafood."

—Executive Chef Holly Smith

Chapter 22

SPOT PRAWN

EXECUTIVE CHEF HOLLY SMITH—CAFE JUANITA

*I*n the North Pacific waters of Alaska, there are five types of shrimp: northern pink, humpy, coonstripe, sidestripe, and spot shrimp. Spot shrimp, also known as "spot prawns," are the largest shrimp in Alaska's waters, reaching lengths of 10 inches. They range from light brown to orange in color with paired spots on their back just behind their head and just in front of their tail—hence the name spot shrimp.

Alaska's commercial shrimp fisheries use two types of harvesting methods: trawling and pot (trap) fishing. Northern pink, humpy, and sidestripe shrimp are caught using trawlers, while coonstripe and spot shrimp are caught using shrimp pots—a more environmentally friendly way of fishing because it reduces bycatch. The basic shrimp trap is made of mesh or wire and is oblong with a conical entrance at each end.

Chef Holly Smith's Northern Italian–inspired cooking at Cafe Juanita and Poco Carretto Gelato has received both local and national acclaim. Chef Smith is the 2008 James Beard Foundation winner for "Best Chef Northwest," and Cafe Juanita has been recognized by *Gourmet Magazine,* Top 50 Restaurants; *Robb Report,* Top 57 Fine Dining; *Wine Spectator,* Best Italian Restaurants; 4 stars from the *Seattle Post-Intelligencer*; and a nomination for "Best Restaurant Service" from the James Beard Foundation 2009.

Chef Smith began her career in Baltimore, then moved on to work at some of the best restaurants in Seattle. In 2000, she opened Cafe Juanita to rave reviews, and in 2008 Poco Carretto Gelato opened. Both restaurants are dedicated to sustainable practices, a commitment to organics, and local sourcing as well as forging relationships with artisan Italian producers.

"I love the versatility of Alaska spot prawns—from simply grilled, butter poached, served raw, or used in sauces and soups—these prawns are incredible. The roe is an amazing prize and makes them not only visually stunning but delicious."

Alaska Spot Prawns with Citrus Risotto

HOW TO MAKE THE CITRUS: Using a sharp paring knife, cut off both ends of the blood oranges, navel orange, lemon, and lime. Do this over a bowl to capture their juice. Remove the peels and piths to expose only the citrus. Following the membrane with the knife, remove the individual segments of the fruit and set aside. Reserve the juice for later.

HOW TO MAKE THE PRAWNS: In a small bowl, add the prawns, chives, and flat-leaf parsley. Season lightly with kosher salt and toss. Set aside.

HOW TO MAKE THE RISOTTO: Peel and dice the onion. Grate the Pecorino. Set aside. In a heavy saucepan, bring the stock to a simmer. In separate heavy saucepan on medium heat, add 3 tablespoons of butter. Add the onion and sauté 3 to 5 minutes until soft and slightly golden. Add the rice and stir to coat with a wooden spoon. Deglaze with the white wine and the reserved citrus juice. Now add the stock, 1 cup at a time, to the rice mixture. The rice will slowly absorb the liquid. After 3 cups of stock have been added, taste the rice for doneness. The rice should be moist, creamy, and just tender. If necessary, add more liquid and cook longer. When done, remove from the heat. Beat in 4 ounces butter. Work quickly until well incorporated. Add the Pecorino cheese. Season with kosher salt. Return the pan to the heat to ensure the cheese is well incorporated. Next, add the seasoned spot prawns. Turn off the heat and gently fold in to cook the prawns, about 1 to 2 minutes.

HOW TO PLATE: Divide the prawn risotto mixture among individual serving plates and top with a drizzle of pumpkin seed oil or balsamic vinegar.

MAKES 4–6 SERVINGS

For the Citrus
2 blood oranges
1 navel orange
1 Meyer lemon
1 lime

For the Prawns
3/4 pound Alaska spot prawns, cleaned and shells removed
2 tablespoons chopped chives
1 tablespoon chopped flat-leaf parsley
Kosher salt, to taste

For the Risotto
1 medium yellow onion
3 ounces Pecorino cheese
6 cups chicken stock (fish stock or vegetable stock may be substituted)
3 tablespoons plus 4 ounces unsalted butter
1 1/4 cups raw carnaroli rice (Italian short-grain rice)
1/4 cup dry white wine
Pumpkin seed oil, for garnish
Balsamic vinegar, for garnish

Grilled Alaska Spot Prawns with Salmoriglio

For the Salmoriglio
3 cloves peeled garlic
1 cup packed fresh marjoram
  leaves (do not substitute
  with oregano)
Zest 2 lemons
1 teaspoon ground cayenne
  pepper, plus more to taste
  as desired
Kosher salt, to taste
2–4 ounces extra-virgin olive
  oil, preferably fruity Italian
  oil
Juice ½ lemon

For the Spot Prawns
1 pound Alaska spot prawns
  (or about 5–7 prawns per
  serving)
Extra-virgin olive oil, as
  needed
Pinch kosher salt
Pinch fresh ground black
  pepper
1 lemon, cut into wedges for
  garnish

HOW TO MAKE THE SALMORIGLIO: Finely mince the garlic and set aside. Finely chop the marjoram. Add the garlic to a cutting board with the marjoram and chop two or three more passes to combine the flavors. In a small bowl, blend the lemon zest, cayenne, and salt with the marjoram and garlic. Drizzle in the extra-virgin olive oil just until a sauce is formed. Add the lemon juice. Taste and adjust with lemon, salt, oil, or cayenne, as necessary. Allow the salmoriglio to sit at room temperature for at least 4 hours. Do not skip this step as the initial flavor is a bit harsh—this will mellow and meld over time. Prior to serving, re-taste and re-season as needed.

HOW TO MAKE THE PRAWNS: Split the prawns through the shell in the middle of their back with a pair of kitchen scissors. Coat the prawns well with extra-virgin olive oil and season with kosher salt and freshly ground black pepper. Grill the prawns over hot coals, about 2 minutes per side, or until slightly opaque.

HOW TO PLATE: Remove the prawns from the grill and divide among individual serving plates. Drizzle the prawns with the salmoriglio and garnish with lemon wedges.

MAKES 4–6 SERVINGS

> "If you buy fresh Alaska spot prawns, two things to consider: If they're alive, cook them immediately. Otherwise, make sure their heads are removed, as whole prawns do not handle well."

SHELLFISH, MOLLUSKS, AND OTHERS

Alaska Spot Prawn Brodetto

For the Satsuma Reduction

1½ cups satsuma juice (any fresh mandarin orange, tangerine, or clementine works well)

Pinch salt

For the Spot Prawn Brodetto

1 medium Yukon gold potato, diced small

6–8 tablespoons unsalted butter

½ fennel bulb, diced small

1 large shallot, finely minced

1 clove garlic, finely minced

Pinch kosher salt, to taste

2 ounces white wine

3 cups crème fraiche

Cayenne pepper, to taste

1 lemon, half zest and half juice

2 pounds Alaska spot prawns, shells removed, roe separated, and meat roughly chopped

Fresh cracked black pepper

3 tablespoons finely chopped chives, for garnish

HOW TO MAKE THE SATSUMA REDUCTION: Combine the satsuma juice with the salt and cook over medium heat. Allow juice to slowly reduce to a thin sauce consistency. The sauce will thicken further as it cools. Season with salt, and if the sauce is too sweet (depends on the fruit), add a dash of lemon or lime juice to accentuate the acidity.

HOW TO MAKE THE SPOT PRAWN BRODETTO: Blanch the Yukon potatoes in boiling salted water. When they're just tender, remove from heat and shock the potatoes in an ice bath to stop the cooking process.

In a medium heavy-bottomed pot, heat 4 tablespoons butter until melted. Add in the fennel bulb and sauté until just tender. Keep the pot on the heat and move the fennel bulb off to one side.

Add 1 tablespoon of butter, if necessary, and add the minced shallot and garlic. Sauté evenly. You want to sauté all the shallots and garlic separate from the fennel bulb to ensure the shallots and garlic are well sweated with no raw garlic flavor, so don't skimp on the butter. When the shallots and garlic are just beginning to turn golden, stir together with the fennel bulb and add the potatoes. Season lightly with the kosher salt, and deglaze the pot with the white wine.

Add the crème fraiche and a tiny pinch of cayenne and bring to a simmer. Taste and adjust the salt. Next, add the lemon zest and, if necessary, some lemon juice. (Note: your crème fraiche will vary in acidity, so adjust for flavor.) Whisk in 2 tablespoons of butter.

Next, prepare the raw spot prawn meat by seasoning it with kosher salt and a little cracked black pepper. Turn off the heat on the soup and stir in the prawn meat. (Note: The prawn meat will be cooked by the heat of the soup and remain very tender and sweet.)

At the last moment, stir in the prawn roe as well. (Note: The roe will need to be removed from the prawns and worked through your fingers to separate. If this step isn't done, there will be strings and clumps of roe.)

HOW TO PLATE: Divide among individual serving dishes and top with a light drizzle of the satsuma reduction. Garnish with the chives and serve immediately.

MAKES 4–6 SERVINGS

Alaska Spot Prawns with Avocado

For the Bread Crumbs

½ loaf bread—ciabatta works well—sliced and dried out in very low-heat oven until completely dry
6 ounces fine quality extra-virgin olive oil (to taste)
3 ounces unsalted butter
Kosher salt
Cayenne pepper

For the Salad

2 ripe avocados
½ pint heirloom cherry tomatoes—cut in half

For the Prawns

1 pound Alaska spot prawns, peeled and deveined
Fresh cracked black pepper
1 tablespoon chopped fresh marjoram
1 tablespoon finely chopped garlic
Juice ½ fresh lemon

TO MAKE THE BREAD CRUMBS: Take the dried bread and pulse in a food processor until fairly small crumbs result. In a large sauté pan, heat 4 ounces extra-virgin olive oil and 1 ounce butter. Add the bread crumbs and toss to coat completely. Over medium heat, cook the bread crumbs until golden, being careful not to burn. Season with kosher salt and cayenne to taste. If more butter is needed to coat the crumbs, add the butter and continue to toss throughout the bread crumbs. Cool the crumbs on a plate. Note: The bread crumbs will hold up to 1 week if no butter is used.

TO MAKE THE SALAD: Cut the avocados in half and remove the pit/seed. Season the avocados lightly with kosher salt and cayenne while still in their skin. Take a large kitchen spoon and scoop out 3 scoops per each half avocado (this keeps it more rustic looking and is easy). Add the halved cherry tomatoes to the bowl with the avocado. The bread crumbs and oil will be tossed with the salad at the last minute to retain the crunch.

TO MAKE THE PRAWNS: Season the prawns well with salt and black pepper. In a large heavy-bottomed sauté pan, heat the remaining butter and oil on medium-high heat. When all the foam/bubbles subside, add the prawns to the pan and allow to brown on one side (don't move them). Add the marjoram and flip the prawns to the other side. At this point, make a space in the pan for the garlic and stir the garlic into the butter and oil mixture. Turn off the heat and allow the prawns to finish cooking off the heat, being careful the garlic doesn't burn.

HOW TO PLATE: Dress the avocado salad on individual serving plates at this time. When the garlic is slightly golden, add the lemon juice and remove from heat. Pour prawns and garlic prawn butter over the avocado salad.

MAKES 4 SERVINGS AS AN APPETIZER, 2–3 SERVINGS AS AN ENTREE

Alaska Spot Prawn Crudo with Sea Urchin, Lime, and Jalapeño on Pumpernickel Crostini

HOW TO MAKE THE CROSTINI: Slice the pumpernickel into thin crostini (2-inch bite size). Drizzle with some extra-virgin olive oil and a light sprinkle of kosher salt. Bake in 375°F oven for 4 to 7 minutes, or until evenly crisped.

HOW TO MAKE THE CRUDO: Cut each prawn in two. In a bowl, dress the prawns with the lime zest, jalapeño, olive oil, and green onion. Season with both kosher salt and sea salt. Adjust the seasoning, if necessary, with lime juice, olive oil (for fruitiness), and salt.

HOW TO PLATE: Place some of the prawn and jalapeño mixture on each crostini and top with one roe of sea urchin (uni). Drizzle some of the liquid from the prawns over the urchin roe and serve with either microgreens or chervil as garnish.

MAKES 4–6 SERVINGS

For the Crostini
½ loaf pumpernickel bread (2-day-old bread is preferable)
Kosher salt, as needed

For the Crudo
1 pound spot prawns, cleaned and shelled
½ lime, zested
3–4 ounces extra-virgin olive oil (fruity is preferred)
1 jalapeño (more based on heat preference) with seeds removed, finely chopped
2 green onions, both white and light green parts, finely sliced
Sea salt, to taste
4–6 sea urchin (uni) roe (found in specialty Asian markets, which sell flats of sashimi-grade urchin roe)
Bunch microgreens or fresh chervil, as garnish

"To keep the roe attached for guests to enjoy, use kitchen scissors to trim a ¼-inch opening on top of the shell. This allows the meat to easily slide out while the roe beneath can be nibbled from the shell. This is finger food at its finest."

"At Passionfish, we buy fish from well-managed, sustainable fisheries. We are dedicated to helping preserve our fish stocks, our fishermen, and our oceans. We won't use an ocean product that we know is poorly harvested, endangered, or from depleted stocks."

—Executive Chef Ted Walter and Cindy Walter

Chapter 23

PACIFIC WEATHERVANE SCALLOPS

EXECUTIVE CHEF TED WALTER AND CINDY WALTER—PASSIONFISH

The Pacific weathervane scallop is one of several species of the true scallops that live in the eastern North Pacific Ocean. Weathervane scallops are found on sand, gravel, and rock bottoms from 25 to 100 fathoms. This scallop supports a sporadic but important commercial fishery in Alaska waters from Yakutat to the eastern Aleutians.

The scallop fishery in Alaska began in 1967 in the Kodiak Island waters and expanded the following year to Yakutat waters. Since then, Cook Inlet, Alaska Peninsula, and eastern Aleutian waters have been explored, and scallop fisheries have decreased. The Alaska scallop fishery has a history of being sporadic due to exploitation of limited stocks, market conditions, and the availability of more lucrative fisheries.

Chef Ted Walter and his wife, Cindy Walter, co-owners of Passionfish restaurant in Pacific Grove, California, are passionate about a sustainable future. Chef Walter incorporates local, sustainable seafood and fresh, local, organic produce into simply inspired meals that are healthy for you and the planet. Chef Walter trained as a classic French chef in restaurants across the country before perfecting his own unique, California culinary style. He returned to his native Monterey County to open Passionfish in 1997; he shops the rich valley farms and the local farmers' markets and buys direct from local fishermen whenever possible. His recipes highlight the fresh flavors of the seasons often enhanced with one of his signature sauces.

Cindy Walter, the daughter of a local fisherman, has made it her mission to take the message of sustainability to the public. Her enthusiastic and positive approach to advocacy has made waves, both locally and nationally. She was named "2008 California Woman of the Year" by California State Assemblyman John Laird in recognition of her advocacy efforts.

"The Alaskan weathervane scallop is very versatile. Their rich flavor is matched with a great textural bite. I can use them interchangeably with just about any recipe I have."

Alaska Weathervane Scallops with Teriyaki Lemongrass Rice

How to make the teriyaki sauce: Combine the garlic, ginger, sugar, and soy sauce in a saucepan and cook on medium heat until the sugar dissolves into the marinade. Remove from heat, and set aside ¼ cup of the marinade for a finishing sauce. Keep the rest to marinade the scallops. Allow the sauce to cool.

How to make the lemongrass rice: Combine the lemongrass, water, and rice. Season and cook the rice until tender.

How to make the scallops: Marinate the scallops in the teriyaki sauce and refrigerate for at least 2 hours. Remove the scallops from the marinade and roast in a glass dish, lightly oiled with vegetable oil in a preheated 500°F oven for 3 minutes.

How to plate: Divide the rice in the centers of four plates. Place the scallops around the rice. Warm ¼ cup of teriyaki sauce in a small saucepan and add drops of the sauce around the plate. Sautéed bok choy is a good accompaniment to this dish.

MAKES 4 SERVINGS

For the Teriyaki Sauce
½ cup chopped garlic
½ cup chopped ginger
2 cups sugar
2 cups soy sauce

For the Lemongrass Rice
2 stalks lemongrass, finely chopped
2 cups water
1 cup jasmine rice, rinsed

For the Scallops
1 pound weathervane scallops

"My best friend Steve came in for dinner a few years ago. He asked me: 'What's the best dish on the menu tonight?' Without hesitating, I replied, 'Alaskan scallops!' Steve immediately told me he really disliked scallops. I looked at him and said, 'Trust me.' He did. 'How did you know I was going to love the scallops?' he later asked. I explained, 'Most scallops are soaked in preservatives, which provide a nasty, metallic-chemical taste. The scallops you are eating tonight are dry-packed with no preservatives.' To this day, I hear Steve telling stories about one of the best dishes he ever ate—Alaskan scallops."

Alaska Weathervane Scallops with Ginger Vinaigrette and Wasabi Slaw

For the Ginger Vinaigrette
2 ounces peeled, chopped ginger
1 ounce peeled, chopped garlic
1 tablespoon sesame oil
½ cup seasoned rice vinegar
2 tablespoons soy sauce
1 tablespoon fish sauce

For the Wasabi Slaw
¼ cup wasabi powder
Water, as needed
1 cup aioli
1 jicama, peeled and shredded
2 unpeeled apples, shredded

For the Scallops
¼ cup flour
1 pound weathervane scallops
Pinch salt to taste
Vegetable oil

How to make the ginger vinaigrette: Sauté the ginger and garlic in sesame oil until fragrant. Stir in the rice vinegar, soy sauce, and the fish sauce. Simmer for 5 minutes, and let cool.

How to make the wasabi slaw: Blend the wasabi powder with just enough water (start with a couple tablespoons) to form a paste. Whisk the paste into the aioli. Stir the shredded jicama and apples into the aioli.

How to make the scallops: Pour the flour in a shallow pan and lightly flour the scallops and season with salt. Pour a small amount of vegetable oil into a cast-iron pan and heat the pan for a few minutes over medium heat. When the pan is hot, place the scallops in the pan and cook for 1½ minutes. Turn the scallops and cook for an additional 1½ minutes. The scallops should appear translucent when cooked to a desired medium-rare.

How to plate: Place the wasabi slaw in the middle of four serving plates. Divide the scallops evenly and place around the slaw. Top the scallops with the ginger vinaigrette.

MAKES 4 SERVINGS

"Always buy 'dry-pack' or 'diver' scallops whenever possible. These are the best of the best."

Alaska Weathervane Scallops with Salmoriglio Sauce and Shaved Summer Squash

For the Summer Squash
2 yellow squash
2 green squash
Olive oil, as needed
Pinch salt and pepper

For the Salmoriglio Sauce
1 bunch fresh oregano
2 tablespoons chopped fresh
   garlic
1/4 cup lemon juice
1 cup olive oil
Salt and pepper to taste

For the Scallops
1 pound weathervane
   scallops
Pinch salt

How to make the squash: Peel the squash lengthwise until you have a bowl full of ribbons. Sauté the squash in olive oil until just tender. Season with salt and pepper, remove from heat, and keep warm.

How to make the salmoriglio sauce: Puree the oregano, garlic, lemon juice, olive oil, and salt and pepper together.

How to make the scallops: Season the scallops with salt. Grill over medium heat for 1½ minutes on each side.

How to plate: Divide the squash among four plates and place the scallops on top. Finish with a drizzling of the sauce.

MAKES 4 SERVINGS

"When preparing scallops, lightly season them with salt and pepper. This allows the natural, rich flavor to be released, making them a joy to eat."

Alaska Weathervane Scallops
and Warm Nicoise Salad with Herb Aioli

HOW TO MAKE THE NICOISE SALAD: In a large, deep frying pan over medium heat, sauté the onion, bell pepper, potatoes, beans, and olives in olive oil. When the bell pepper softens, add the red wine and fish stock. Reduce by half over medium heat. Add the basil, and season to taste with salt and pepper.

HOW TO MAKE THE SCALLOPS: Grill the scallops approximately 1½ minutes on each side over medium-high heat.

HOW TO PLATE: Toss the nicoise salad with the aioli and divide among four plates. Top each salad with several scallops.

MAKES 4 SERVINGS

For the Nicoise Salad
2 red onions, diced
1 red bell pepper, sliced and diced
8 medium-size red potatoes, steamed and quartered
20 yellow wax beans, steamed
40 nicoise olives
2 tablespoons olive oil
½ cup red wine
½ cup fish stock
¼ cup basil puree
Pinch salt and pepper

For the Scallops
1 pound weathervane scallops
¼ cup herb aioli

"We are working towards a future where we will not only be serving fish farmed on land, but we'll have an abundance of wild products from the ocean."

Alaskan Weathervane Scallop Chowder

¼ pound bacon, diced
2 onions, chopped
4 cloves garlic, chopped
3 cups fish stock
3 cups cream
Pinch salt and pepper
4 potatoes, peeled and diced
1 pound weathervane
  scallops
2 tablespoons chopped
  thyme
2 tablespoons chopped
  parsley

HOW TO MAKE THE CHOWDER: In a large, deep pan over medium heat, sauté the bacon until crisp. Add the onions and garlic and continue to sauté until soft. Add the fish stock and cream. Season with salt and pepper. Add the potatoes and continue cooking until the potatoes are soft. Taste and season with more salt and pepper if needed. Add the scallops and thyme. Cook another 5 minutes, stirring occasionally. Add the parsley.

HOW TO PLATE: Ladle the chowder into four bowls, and serve immediately.

MAKES 4 SERVINGS

"Never overcook scallops, or they will become hard and rubbery."

Acknowledgments

*J*ames O. Fraioli would like to thank the following: Jessica-Nicosia Nadler (www
.jessicanicosia.com); Chef John Hall and the extraordinary culinary team at Le
Cordon Bleu College of Culinary Arts—Sacramento, including Chef Michael Cross and
Chef Jessica Williams, as well as Chef Adrian Day-Murchison, Chef Bruno Caccia, Chef
Sandra Washington, Chef Robert Siegmund, Chef Dave Nelson, Chef Nichol Santiste-
ven, Rose Davila, Tony Mora, and Andrew D. Pugh-Gomes; Laura Flemming of the
Alaska Seafood Marketing Institute (www.alaskaseafood.org); Jim Trujillo of Ed's Kasi-
lof Seafoods (www.kasilofseafoods.com); the Alaska Division of Tourism; the Monterey
Bay Aquarium's Seafood Watch Program; Mary Norris at Globe Pequot Press; Andrea
Hurst of Andrea Hurst Literary Management; and, last but certainly not least, Chef John
Ash and all the contributing chefs. Without their wonderful support and assistance, this
book would not have been possible.

Additional Photography Credits

Metric Conversion Tables

METRIC U.S. APPROXIMATE EQUIVALENTS

Liquid Ingredients		Dry Ingredients	
METRIC	U.S. MEASURES	METRIC	U.S. MEASURES
1.23 ML	¼ TSP.	2 (1.8) G	$\frac{1}{16}$ OZ.
2.36 ML	½ TSP.	3½ (3.5) G	⅛ OZ.
3.70 ML	¾ TSP.	7 (7.1) G	¼ OZ.
4.93 ML	1 TSP.	15 (14.2) G	½ OZ.
6.16 ML	1¼ TSP.	21 (21.3) G	¾ OZ.
7.39 ML	1½ TSP.	25 G	⅞ OZ.
8.63 ML	1¾ TSP.	30 (28.3) G	1 OZ.
9.86 ML	2 TSP.	50 G	1¾ OZ.
14.79 ML	1 TBSP.	60 (56.6) G	2 OZ.
29.57 ML	2 TBSP.	80 G	2⅘ OZ.
44.36 ML	3 TBSP.	85 (84.9) G	3 OZ.
59.15 ML	¼ CUP	100 G	3½ OZ.
118.30 ML	½ CUP	115 (113.2) G	4 OZ.
236.59 ML	1 CUP	125 G	4½ OZ.
473.18 ML	2 CUPS OR 1 PT.	150 G	5¼ OZ.
709.77 ML	3 CUPS	250 G	8⅞ OZ.
946.36 ML	4 CUPS OR 1 QT.	454 G	1 LB. OR 16 OZ.
3.79 L	4 QTS. OR 1 GAL.	500 G	1 LIVRE OR 17⅗ OZ.

Index

About the Author

*J*ames O. Fraioli (pronounced "fray-o-lee") is a full-time cookbook writer. He is the published author of 17 titles, with additional books currently in production. Seasoned, skilled, and recognized for both the speed and grace of his writing, Fraioli's cookbooks have garnered numerous literary and design awards, and have appeared on dozens of national radio shows, including *Martha Stewart Living Radio, Food Talk with Rocco DiSpirito, The Gene Burns Show,* and *The Tom Douglas Show.* The author is notorious for teaming up with celebrity chefs and world-renowned restaurants to showcase the best the culinary world has to offer. Participating chefs over the years include James Beard award-winners John Ash, Tom Douglas, Bradley Ogden, and Jacques Pepin, as well as Emeril Lagasse and Roy Yamaguchi. Fraioli's cookbooks have also been featured on the Food Network, *The Ellen DeGeneres Show,* and given as gifts to members of the White House staff. Fraioli's beautiful and well-crafted books, continually noted for their exceptional prose, high-production value, exquisite photography, and savory subject matter, have received further praise from such esteemed periodicals as *Forbes Traveler,* the *San Francisco Chronicle* and the *New York Times.*

Prior to his successful book-writing career, Fraioli served as a contributing writer and editor for more than 20 magazine publications, and has more than 250 feature articles to his credit.